Welcome to  xtb Issue Eleven

Write & Wrong

...e
...nd...

- Check out <u>who</u> Jesus is and <u>why</u> He came in **John's Gospel**
- Meet the last kings of Israel, and find out why the Israelites had to leave their homes in the books of **2 Kings, Isaiah** and **Jeremiah**.

Are you ready to explore the Bible? Fill in the bookmark...
...then turn over the page to start exploring with XTB!

Table Talk FOR FAMILIES

Look out for **Table Talk** — a book to help children and adults explore the Bible together. It can be used by:

- Families
- One adult with one child
- Children's leaders with their groups
- Any other way you want to try

Table Talk uses the same Bible passages as XTB so that they can be used together if wanted. You can buy Table Talk from your local Christian bookshop—or call us on **0333 123 0880** to order a copy.

This book belongs to

....

Sometimes I'm called

...............................(nickname)

My birthday is

....

My age is

....

I like to write (stories? jokes? letters? emails? poems? ...)

....

....

How to find your way around the Bible.

**Look out for the READ sign.
It tells you what Bible bit to read.**

**READ
2 Kings 2v7-15**

**So, if the notes say... READ 2 Kings 2v7-15
...this means chapter 2 and verses 7 to 15
...and this is how you find it.**

Use the **Contents** page in your Bible to
find where 2 Kings begins.

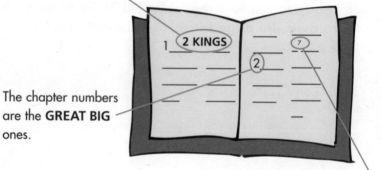

The chapter numbers
are the **GREAT BIG**
ones.

The verse numbers are the
tiny ones!

**Oops! Keep getting lost?
Cut out this bookmark and use it to keep your place.**

How to use xtb

1.  Find a time and place when you can read the Bible each day.

2.  Get your Bible, a pencil and your XTB notes.

3.  Ask God to help you to understand what you read.

4.  Read today's XTB page and Bible bit.

5.  Pray about what you have read and learnt.

6. If you can, talk to an adult or a friend about what you've learnt.

Your Free XTB Writing Pad

This copy of XTB comes with a free **XTB Writing Pad**.

That's why this issue of XTB is called '**Write and Wrong**'. We'll see how many of the kings of Israel lived **wrong** lives; we'll find out why so many people had the **wrong** idea about Jesus; and we'll **write** about what we discover—in letters, lists, and on a paper plane! (*Check out Day 50 to find out more about the plane...*)

Are you ready to try out your XTB Writing Pad? Then hurry on to Day 1.

TWO BY TWO

How many times can you spot the number **two** on these <u>two</u> pages? _____

*Now crack the code to find out why there are so many **two**'s around...*

TWO KINGDOMS

God's people, the Israelites, had split into two kingdoms.

1 The ***northern*** kingdom was called

___ ___ ___ ___ ___ ___ .

Its capital city was ___ ___ ___ ___ ___ ___ ___ .

2 The ***southern*** kingdom was called

___ ___ ___ ___ ___ .

Its capital was ___ ___ ___ ___ ___ ___ ___ ___ .

Check out the two kingdoms on the map.

Flag Code

= A
= D
= E
= H
= I
= J
= L
= M
= N
= O
= P
= R
= S
= T
= U
= V

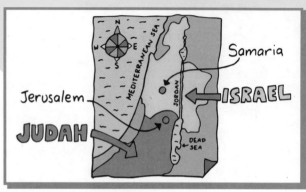

TWO KINDS OF KING

The kings of Israel and Judah came in two kinds:

1 Kings who ___ ___ ___ ___ ___ God and obeyed His laws.

2 Kings who turned away from God and served

___ ___ ___ ___ ___ ___ ___ gods (statues) instead.

Turn to the next page to find out more.

DAY 1
CONTINUED

TWO OF A KIND

xtb 2 Kings 2v11

TWO PROPHETS

God spoke to His people—and their kings—through His prophets (God's messengers).

1 In the book of 1 Kings we met the
■■□■●□▬■◄■

fiery prophet __ __ __ __ __ __.

Elijah spoke God's Word to the Israelites, telling them to turn away from pretend gods and turn back to God.

Amazingly, Elijah didn't die! God was so pleased with him, that He took Elijah up to heaven! *Read the passage to find out how.*

READ
2 Kings 2v11

How did Elijah go to heaven? *Write or draw your answer here.*

2 Elijah's servant took over as God's prophet.
■■□■●□▬■□◄

His name was __ __ __ __ __ __.

In the next few days we'll read about how God used Elisha to do amazing things.

THINK SPOT

God spoke to His people through His two prophets, Elijah and Elisha. They told the people to turn back to God, and how to love and serve Him. Today, **God speaks** to His people (Christians) through His Word, the <u>Bible</u>. Copy the prayer below onto a page from your **XTB Writing Pad**. Keep it in your Bible, and pray it each day before doing XTB.

PRAY

Dear God, thank you for giving me your Word, the Bible, so that I can know You better and better. Please help me to understand what I read, and to obey what You tell me. Amen

DAY 2 OODLES OF OIL

Elisha was God's prophet (messenger). God used Elisha to look after a lady who was in loads of trouble...

READ
2 Kings 4v1

This woman's husband had died. She couldn't pay the money he owed, and no-one else would. It looked as though she would lose both of her sons!

How do you think she felt? *Draw her face.*

The woman went to God's prophet, Elisha, for help...

READ
2 Kings 4v2-7

What did the woman have? (v2)
- **a)** A little food.
- **b)** A little oil.
- **c)** A little kitten.

What did Elisha tell her to collect? (v3)

Loads of _____

The widow only had a <u>little</u> oil. How many of the jars did she fill? (v6)

None / A few / Six / All

Wow! God turned her <u>little</u> bit of oil into <u>oodles</u> of oil!

Draw her face now.

God cares for those who no one else cares for. <u>We</u> can follow His example.

Copy all of the <u>red letters</u> (in order) to see one of God's commands to us.

L _ _ _ _   _ _ _ _ _ _

_ _ _ _ _ _ _ _   _ _ _ _

_ _ _ _ _ _

This command is in James 1v27.

THINK+PRAY

How can <u>you</u> care for those who need help? Maybe by befriending an old lady who has no family. Or regularly giving money to a charity that cares for people. Or... What can you do?

_____

_____

Ask God to help you do this.

Tearfund are a Christian charity who help out people without food, money or homes. You can find out about them from their website at www.tearfund.org

What do you like about your bedroom?

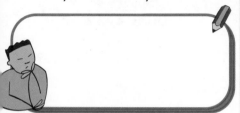

Elisha didn't have his own room, because he travelled about so much. But that was about to change...

READ
2 Kings 4v8-10

Yesterday we saw how God used Elisha to look after a widow and her sons. Now God used another woman to look after Elisha! What did she give Elisha every time he was in the area? (v8)

Then what did she build for Elisha? (v10)

Wow! That was so-o-o kind! She showed her love for God by being kind to Elisha.

Elisha wanted to do something for her as a thank you...

READ
2 Kings 4v11-17

Fill in the gaps from v16.

About this time next **y**_____, you will hold a **s**_____ in your **a**_____.

The woman didn't want to get her hopes up.

Man of God, don't lie to me!

But Elisha was serious about thanking this woman, and he knew that God could give her a baby.

Did God give her a son? (v17)

Yes / No

PRAY

Wow! God is so-o-o kind to His people. What can <u>you</u> thank Him for right now?

This woman did a lot for Elisha. Think of someone who has done a lot for <u>you</u>. Use your XTB Writing Pad to write to them and say a BIG thank you.

xtb · 2 Kings 4v18-37

Remember the woman who built a room for Elisha? God gave her and her husband a surprise present—a baby! But that's not the end of the story...

Some years later, at harvest time, the boy went out one morning to join his father.

Suddenly, he cried out.

My head! My head!

Carry him to his mother.

The boy sat on his mother's lap until midday, and then he died.

She carried him up to Elisha's room, and put him on the bed.

Send a servant with a donkey.

I need to go to see Elisha.

She went as fast as she could to Mount Carmel, where Elisha was.

When Elisha heard her news, he spoke to his servant, Gehazi.

Hurry! Take my stick and go.

Go straight to the house and hold my stick over the boy.

Gehazi held Elisha's stick over the boy...

...but there was no sign of life.

Taken from 2 Kings 4v18-31.

READ
2 Kings 4v32-37

What was the first thing Elisha did? (v33)

He p_____

Then Elisha laid down on the boy's body—twice. What did the boy do? (v35)

He **s**_____ seven times and opened his **e**_____.

Wow! God answered Elisha's prayers and brought the boy back to life!!

THINK+PRAY

We can talk to God about anything. <u>Nothing</u> is too hard for Him! He won't always answer our prayers in the way we expect—but He will always do what's right and good. What do you want to talk to Him about now?

DAY 5 POT OF... DEATH!

What would you do with a bag of flour?

Yesterday, I used flour to make chocolate brownies. (Yum!) But Elisha used flour in a very different way...

READ
2 Kings 4v38-40

 the correct answers.

There was a famine in the land, so there wasn't enough **food/wine/paper**. Elisha told his servant to cook a big pot of **porridge/soup/stew**. One of the men found a wild **boar/vine/radish**, and picked some of its gourds (fruit). He chopped up the **grapes/gourds/guards** and put them in the stew. When the men began to eat they cried out, 'There is **poison/death/dandruff** in the pot!' And they could not **eat/drink/wear** it!

The stew was poisonous! It looked like they would have to throw it away—even though there was a famine. But Elisha, God's prophet, had other ideas...

READ
2 Kings 4v41

What did Elisha put in the stew?

Flour (meal) is pretty ordinary. You can't do much with it except bake (or make flour bombs!). But after the flour was added, the poisonous stew was good to eat. Why do you think this was?

a) The flour was special.
b) Elisha was special.
c) _____ was special.

PRAY

The special person in this story is God! It was **God** who used ordinary flour to make that deadly stew safe. We can always talk to God about our problems. And He may well use something ordinary to sort things out for us. Talk to Him now.

DAY 6 SIGNPOSTS

Miracles are like **signposts**. We've read about three so far:
1. The little bit of oil that turned into oodles of oil. (Day 2)
2. The dead boy who was brought back to life. (Day 4)
3. The poisonous stew that was made good to eat. (Day 5)

These miracles all pointed to who Elisha was—He was **God's messenger**. It was God's power, but Elisha spoke for Him.

Now for another miracle...

READ
2 Kings 4v42-44

There was a famine where Elisha was, so this man had brought food. How much food did he bring? (v42)

_____ **loaves of barley bread**

How many hungry men were there? (v43) _____ **men**

The loaves of bread would have been small—nothing like enough to feed 100 men! But what had **God** said? (v43)

> They will eat and have some
> _____ _____

xtb   2 Kings 4v42-44

Did God's words come true? (v44)   **Yes / No**

Hmm... That reminds me of another story.

Who else fed a hungry crowd with a tiny amount of food?

_____

Did you know?

Jesus fed a HUGE crowd (5000 men, plus women and children) with one boy's packed lunch! *You can read this story in John 6v5-13.*

The miracle **Elisha** did showed that he spoke for God. The miracle **Jesus** did showed that He was God!!!

THINK + PRAY

All these miracles showed people that Elisha was God's messenger. So they should listen to him. And we should listen even more to Jesus! Remember your prayer from Day 1? Ask God to help you listen to His Word, the Bible, and do what He says.

DAY 7

MR COOL & MISS NOBODY

 2 Kings 5v1-8

Meet Mr Cool:

Actually, his name is Naaman. But as you'll see, he's a cool guy...

READ
2 Kings 5v1

Which of these describes Naaman?
a) army commander
b) highly respected
c) brave soldier

They _all_ describe him! Naaman really is Mr Cool, except...

Take the first letter of each pic.

Naaman had _ _ _ _ _ _ _

Leprosy is a nasty disease where your skin goes all lumpy and falls off. Nobody could cure Naaman's leprosy.

Meet Miss Nobody:

This slave girl was an Israelite. She had been captured by Naaman's people and now worked for Naaman's wife. We don't even know her name—but **she** knew something very important...

READ
2 Kings 5v2-8

The slave girl knew that God could cure Naaman's leprosy. Who did she tell Naaman to go and see? (v3)

The **p**_____ in Samaria.

She meant _ _ _ _ _ _ _

Check the map on **Day 1** to see where Samaria was.

• **Mr Cool** couldn't heal himself—he needed help.
• The **king of Israel** didn't help—he just panicked! (v7)
• **Miss Nobody** knew that _God_ could heal Naaman, and she told him where to go to get help.

THINK+PRAY

Do you ever feel like a 'nobody', like that slave girl? You're probably young, like she was. And I guess you're not a king or army commander! But _you_ can do what she did, and tell people how they can find out more about God. Use your XTB Writing Pad to make a list of ways your friends can find out about God. (_Eg: at church, a Christian group, by reading the Bible..._) Now ask God to help you tell one of your friends how to find out more.

Yesterday, we met **Mr Cool**—an important man called Naaman. *Cross out the **X**'s to see what Naaman brought with him to Israel.*

XHOXRXSXESX
XCHXARIXOXTSX
XSXILXVEXRX
XXGXOLXXDX
XFXINXEX
XCLXOTXHXESX

You can see that Naaman was a very important man! But he had a problem. What was it?

> He had L_____

An Israelite slave girl said that **Elisha**, God's prophet, could cure Naaman. So Naaman went to see Elisha. But when he arrived at Elisha's house, Elisha <u>didn't</u> come out to meet him!

READ
2 Kings 5v9-12

Elisha sent a servant to Naaman. What was Elisha's message? (v10)

> Go and wash yourself **s**_____ times in the River **J**_____ and you will be healed.

How did Naaman feel? (v11)
a) Pleased
b) Angry
c) Bored

Naaman was furious! Why should he wash in the Jordan? Surely God would cure him in a magical, spectacular way—not by dunking in a muddy river!

He wasn't going to do what Elisha said. But his servants were much wiser...

READ
2 Kings 5v13-14

Naaman's servants persuaded him to wash in the Jordan as he'd been told. What happened? (v14)

a) He was cured
b) He was cold
c) He was curried

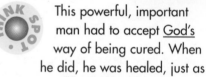

THINK SPOT

This powerful, important man had to accept <u>God's</u> way of being cured. When he did, he was healed, just as God's messenger had said.

PRAY

Obeying God's words, and living His way, is <u>always</u> the best thing to do—even if His words seem surprising. Ask God to help you to **trust** what He says in the Bible, and **obey** His words, no matter how hard (or odd!) that seems.

DAY 9 A CHANGED MAN

Crack the code to fill in the speech bubble.

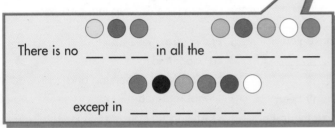

There is no _ _ _ in all the _ _ _ _ _

except in _ _ _ _ _ _.

Who do you think is speaking?
a) An Israelite
b) Elisha
c) An enemy of Israel

These words were spoken by Naaman, the commander of an enemy army! Naaman came from Aram, where they believed in a pretend god called Rimmon. But when Naaman was cured of his leprosy, he realised that **God** is the One true God.

READ
2 Kings 5v15-19

Naaman had loads of silver, gold and fine clothes with him. Did Elisha accept them? (v16)

Yes / No

2 Kings 5v15-19

What did Naaman ask for?
a) Elisha's autograph
b) Some food for his journey
c) Some earth to take with him

How odd! Maybe Naaman thought he could only pray to <u>Israel's God</u> if he stood on some of <u>Israel's soil</u>! If so, he was wrong. We can pray to God **anywhere**, **anytime**.

Think back to the slave girl who told Naaman to go and see Elisha. Her master came home a changed man. Not only was he cured of his leprosy, but he had become a follower of the One true God. How do you think she felt?

THINK + PRAY
Do you follow Jesus? Tell others about Him, and they could become Christians too. They'll live with you in heaven and you'll have done something everlasting. What a great way to live! Ask God to help you.

As Naaman was leaving in his chariot, Elisha's servant Gehazi chased after him.

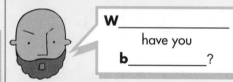

Elisha says, 'Two young men have just come to me. Please give them some silver and two sets of clothes.'

Naaman was happy to help, and even gave Gehazi <u>more</u> than he asked for.

Sounds great, doesn't it? Just one small problem. Greedy Gehazi was lying!!!

READ
2 Kings 5v19-27

What did Elisha ask Gehazi? (v25)

W_____
have you
b_____?

Gehazi pretended he hadn't been anywhere, but Elisha knew the truth.

How was Gehazi punished for his greed? (v27)
- **a)** He got away with it
- **b)** He had to pay Naaman back
- **c)** He caught Naaman's leprosy

Copy the <u>blue</u> letters from Gehazi's bags.

G ___ ___   ___ ___ ___ ___ ___

___ ___ ___ ___   ___ ___ ___ ___ ___

The Bible tells us that **God** gives us everything we have. He gives us <u>good</u> gifts. **If we steal**, it's like telling God, 'You haven't given me enough. I need more!'

If we steal, it shows that we don't <u>trust</u> God to give us everything we need.

Have you ever...
- **a)** shoplifted?
- **b)** borrowed something and not returned it?
- **c)** taken stuff you weren't supposed to?
- **d)** dodged a bus fare?

THINK SPOT

If we do any of these things we cheat and hurt others—AND GOD!

If you have stolen anything, say **sorry** to God. Ask Him to help you to change.

PRAY **Thank** God for the good things He has given you. Ask Him to help you to trust Him for everything you need.

(Circle) the things that **float**.

I guess you included the beach ball, and the duck. But what about the axe? An iron axe doesn't float—or does it???

Elisha was the leader of a group of prophets (God's messengers). But their meeting hall was starting to get overcrowded...

READ
2 Kings 6v1-7

What happened to the axe-head?
a) it melted in the sun
b) it fell into the water
c) a crocodile ate it

Why was the guy so upset?
a) he'd borrowed it
b) it was his favourite axe
c) he'd lost his rubber duck

In those days an iron axe-head was expensive. So losing it really mattered.

What did Elisha do?
a) told the man off
b) pushed him in the river
c) made the axe-head float

Sometimes, Bible stories can be hard to understand.
• An older Christian may be able to explain it.
• Or another part of the Bible may tell you about it.
But sometimes we **don't know** why something happened!

*In that case, the best thing to do is think carefully about what we **do know**. So let's try that now:*

1. Who were the people in the story? **a)** God's enemies
b) God's followers

2. What is God like? **a)** He is kind and loving
b) He is cruel and mean

3. What can God do? **a)** He can do anything
b) He can only do some things

The answers are **b,a,a**. God can do **anything**, so making iron float is easy for Him. And God loves to be **kind** to His followers. Maybe that's why He made the axe-head float, because He cared about the man's sadness.

PRAY

God loves to be kind to **you** too. Use your XTB Writing Pad to write a thank you letter to God, thanking Him for His HUGE kindness to you.

Answers: apple, beach ball, boat & rubber duck.

DAY 12 WHO'S THE KING?

Being king probably feels pretty powerful. But the king of Aram (Syria) was about to find out that he didn't have much power at all...

The king of Aram went to war against Israel. **R**

He made plans to attack God's people, the Israelites.

But his plans didn't work out... **E**

...because Elisha kept warning the king of Israel!

The king of Aram was furious! **A**

Find out where Elisha is, so that I can capture him.

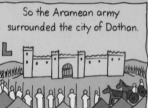

So the Aramean army surrounded the city of Dothan. **L**

Elisha's servant was scared when he saw the army. **K**

What shall we do?

But Elisha told him not to be afraid. **I**

Those who are with *us* are more than those who are with *them*.

Then Elisha asked God to show his servant the truth. **N**

O Lord, open his eyes so that he may see.

And the servant saw the hills full of horses and chariots of fire! **G**

Read the verses to see what happened next.

READ
2 Kings 6v18-23

Circle the correct answers.

Elijah/Elisha prayed that the enemy soldiers would become **blind/blue**. Then he led them to the city of **Edinburgh/Samaria**. God opened their **bags/eyes** again so that they could see. Elisha told the **queen/king** of Israel not to **kill/cuddle** them. Instead, the soldiers were given a great **cabbage/feast** before leaving.

The king of Aram <u>thought</u> he was in control, but he wasn't! *Copy the letters hidden in the cartoon story (in order) to see why.*

God is the

_ _ _ _ _   _ _ _ _ _

 PRAY

God is the King of everything. He is always in control. Thank Him for this.

DAY 13 — THE SIEGE OF SAMARIA

xtb 2 Kings 6v24–7v2

Yesterday, we saw that **God** is the

R_____ K_____.

That means that God is in control, and that His words always come true.

Today we'll meet three people who need to learn that:

1. The king of Aram

Ben-Hadad, king of Aram, attacked Israel and its capital city Samaria...

READ
2 Kings 6v24-25

Did you know?

A **siege** is when an army circles a castle or walled city to trap the people inside it. When the food runs out, the people have to surrender—or starve!

The people in Samaria were starving. Food had become terribly expensive. Even a donkey's **h_____** cost 80 pieces of **s_____**! (v25)

2. The king of Israel

The king of Israel was trapped inside Samaria too. When he saw how much the people were suffering, he blamed Elisha, and even planned to kill him! (v26-33) But Elisha had a message for the king.

READ
2 Kings 7v1-2

Elisha said there'd be plenty of cheap food in Samaria again. When would that happen? (v1)

a) in a few days
b) tomorrow
c) in two weeks

---

3. The Israelite officer

This officer was the messenger for the king of Israel. But he <u>didn't believe</u> Elisha! So what did Elisha tell him about the promised food? (v2)

You will **s_____** it, but you will not **e_____** any of it.

Elisha wasn't speaking his own words. Whose words was he speaking? (v1)

The L_____'s

PRAY

Elisha was speaking **God's** words, but the king's messenger didn't believe him. Do <u>you</u> sometimes find it hard to believe God's words in the Bible? *Copy all the red letters here:*

_ _ _ _ _ _ _ _ _ _

Now **ask God** to help you do this!

DAY 14 GOOD NEWS!

The story so far:

- The Arameans have attacked **Israel**.
- The city of Samaria is under **siege**, and its people are **starving**.
- **Elisha** has said there'll be plenty of cheap **food** tomorrow. This was **God's** promise.
- But the king of Israel, and his messenger, <u>don't</u> **believe** Elisha.

*Find the **yellow** words in the wordsearch.*

G	O	I	S	R	A	E	L
O	D	A	H	S	I	L	E
S	T	A	R	V	I	N	G
D	O	O	F	G	O	D	S
S	I	E	G	E	N	E	W
E	V	E	I	L	E	B	S

That evening, four men with leprosy decided to leave the city and go to the enemy camp...

READ
2 Kings 7v3-11

What did the men find when they reached the enemy camp? (v5)

a) loads of Aramean soldiers
b) no one
c) a circus tent

Why had the Arameans left? (v6)

a) they were fed up with fighting
b) God made them hear the sound of a large army
c) God made them hear music

For a while, the men grabbed everything they could. But then they went back to the city to tell everyone else their news. *Fill in the gaps from v9.*

We have **g**_____ **n**_____ and we shouldn't keep it to **o**_____.

Copy the leftover letters from the wordsearch to see what they spell.

_ _ _ _ _   _ _ _ _

These four men had **good news** to share. They knew it would be wrong to keep it to themselves. If you're a Christian (a follower of Jesus) then <u>you</u> have good news to share too! The good news that Jesus came as our Rescuer, so that we can be friends with God. *More about this on Day 21.*

PRAY

Do you still have the list you wrote on Day 7? It will give you some ideas for how you can share the good news about Jesus with your friends. Ask God to help you do that this week.

(Circle) the correct answers.

The people in **Samaria/Scotland** were **dancing/starving** because of the siege. God had said there'd be plenty of cheap **chocolate/food** tomorrow. The **king/queen** of Israel and his messenger **did/didn't** believe it. **Five/Four** men had gone to the enemy camp and found it empty! They came to the city to share their **good/bad** news.

The four men told their good news that the enemy army had gone. But the king of Israel didn't believe it! He thought the Arameans were trying to trick him...

READ
2 Kings 7v12-16

Had the Arameans gone away? (v15)
Yes / No

Was there plenty of cheap food? (v16)
Yes / No

Fit all of your answers (including the two 'Yes's from above) into the puzzle.

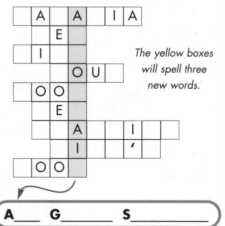

The yellow boxes will spell three new words.

A___ G_____ S_____

God **promised** that there'd be plenty of cheap food for His people to eat—and there was. *Just as God said!*

But God had given a **warning** as well—to the king's messenger who didn't believe God's promise.

> You will **see** it, but you will not **eat** any of it.

READ
2 Kings 7v17-20

Did God's warning come true? (v16)
Yes / No

PRAY

God's words **always** come true—His promises <u>and</u> His warnings. How does that make you feel? Talk to God about it now—and remember that you can always trust God to do what's right and good.

Welcome back to John's book about Jesus. In it we'll see Jesus ride a donkey, make a blind man see and raise a friend back to life! And we'll also read some of the amazing things Jesus said.

READ
John 20v31

Why did John write his book? Go forward one letter to fill in the missing words. (A=B, B=C, C=D etc)

So that you may _ _ _ _ _ _ _ _ _
             A D K H D U D

that _ _ _ _ _ _ is the Christ
     I D R T R

(Messiah), the _ _ _ of _ _ _',
               R N M   F N C

and that by believing you may have

_ _ _ _ in His name.
K H E D

John wants us to believe that Jesus is the Christ (Messiah). That means God's chosen King.

In his book, John tells us loads of amazing things that Jesus did and said.

They are all *signposts* pointing to who Jesus is. They help us understand more about Jesus.

PRAY

Thank God that you can read all about Jesus in John's book. Ask God to help you to learn loads about Jesus and to understand who He really is.

Turn to the next page now!

READ
John 9v1-4

Jesus and His disciples passed a blind man. The disciples thought blindness was a punishment from God. So they asked Jesus...

> Was it something he did wrong or was it his parents?

Complete Jesus's answer (v3).

> Neither he nor his parents sinned to cause his blindness. It happened so that _____
> _____

Jesus was going to do something amazing for him so people could see **God** at work!

READ
John 9v5

In the speech bubble draw a picture to show what Jesus claimed.

> **I am the**
>
> **of the world.**

If we don't know and love Jesus it's like we are **blind**. We **can't see** that we've sinned and need Jesus to **forgive** us. Jesus is the **light** who shows us the way to be forgiven. (more about that on Day 19).

READ
John 9v6-7

Wow! The man obeyed what Jesus told him to do, and he was able to see!

PRAY If people trust Jesus and do what He says they can have their sins forgiven! Thank Jesus that He can cure illness and forgive our horrible sin.

 John 9v8-23

People have all sorts of ideas about who Jesus is...

> **Jesus is God's Son who can rescue us from sin!**

> **No he's not! He was just a good man who said great things.**

Jesus has made a blind man see. Everyone who knew the man wanted to know who had healed him (John 9v8-12). But the Pharisees (Jewish leaders) were not so excited about Jesus...

The Pharisees disagreed with each other about who Jesus was. *Fill in the missing a*s, *e*s and *o*s to reveal what they said (v16).

READ
John 9v13-17

> **This m__n is n__t fr__m G__d for he does not k__ __p the S__bb__th.**

They said that Jesus wasn't sent by God because He worked on God's rest day (*Sabbath*). But doing good and healing someone on the Sabbath wasn't wrong! So some Pharisees thought Jesus was a **good man**.

A pr__ph__t (v17)
The healed man thought that Jesus was a messenger sent by God. He was half right! But he didn't yet realise that Jesus was the special King sent by God to rescue His people.

Most of the Pharisees refused to believe that Jesus was sent by God, even after they had spoken to the healed man's parents (it's in verses 18-23).

THINK + PRAY

Who do YOU think Jesus is?

_____

If you believe that God sent Jesus to rescue you, thank God for sending Jesus.

DAY 18 BLINDING TRUTH

The Pharisees (religious leaders) are still questioning the man who Jesus cured of blindness. They want to prove that Jesus was **not** sent by God.

READ
John 9v24-27

What did the Pharisees want the man to say Jesus was (v24)? Tick one!

a saviour	☐
a sinner	☐
a swimmer	☐

The man refused to say that Jesus was a sinner. All he knew was that Jesus had done an amazing thing for him.

What did he ask them (v27)?

Do you want to become his disciples?	☐
Do you want to become disco dancers?	☐
Do you want a dishwasher?	☐

He asked them if they wanted to become Jesus' followers! This made the Pharisees steaming mad!

READ
John 9v28-34

Who did the Pharisees follow (v28)?

Jesus	☐
Maureen	☐
Moses	☐

They knew that Moses was sent by God, but didn't believe that Jesus was too.

Who did the healed man say had sent Jesus (v33)?

Moses	☐
God	☐
The Pharisees	☐

Brilliant! This guy worked out that Jesus must be from God, because He could do things that only **God** could do. Sadly the Pharisees refused to believe the evidence.

PRAY

Do you believe that Jesus was sent by God? Then ask God to help you live in a way that pleases Jesus.

DAY 19 THE BIG CHOICE

The Pharisees threw the healed man out of the synagogue. So Jesus went to find him...

READ
John 9v35-38

Use the **flag code** to reveal what Jesus said (v35).

Do you believe in the

__ __ __ __ __ __ ___?

The **Son of Man** is the name Jesus called Himself. Jesus is **God**, but He became a **man** so that He could die for us and **rescue** us from our sinful ways.

What did the man say (v38)?

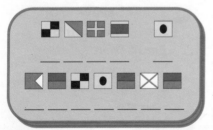

That's how we should respond to Jesus. We should believe Him and worship Him by living His way.

Flag Code

= A
= B
= D
= E
= F
= G
= I
= L
= M
= N
= O
= R
= S
= V

READ
John 9v39-41

I have come into the world so that the blind will see and those who see will become blind.

The Pharisees thought they could **see**. They thought they knew the truth about God. But they didn't because they refused to **see** that **Jesus is God**.

But some people realise they are blind and need Jesus to rescue them from their blind sinful ways.

PRAY

There are only two choices. Believe in Jesus and live His way. Or have nothing to do with Jesus. Which will you choose? Ask God to help you make the right choice.

DAY 20 — GREAT GATE!

Today Jesus says He is both a shepherd and a gate!

READ
John 10v1-6

1. JESUS THE SHEPHERD

Who will the sheep listen to (v3)?

the shepherd ☐
the thief ☐

Will they ever follow a stranger (v5)?

yes, sometimes ☐
no, never! ☐

Some religious leaders (like the Pharisees) tried to lead people away from God. Like a thief trying to take sheep the wrong way.

But true followers of Jesus will only follow <u>Him</u>. He shows them the right way to live. They won't follow anyone else.

2. JESUS THE GATE

READ
John 10v7-10

Look at the sheep pen picture.

How many ways into the sheep pen are there?

You can only get in through the **gate**. It is the **only way**.

Jesus, the gate, is the **ONLY WAY** to become friends with God. The **ONLY WAY** to be saved (have your sins forgiven—v9). The **ONLY WAY** to eternal **life** in heaven (v10).

PRAY

Read through the last box again, one sentence at a time, thanking Jesus for each great truth about Him!

DAY 21 **THE GOOD SHEPHERD**

John 10V11-15

We're thinking about sheep. No, not lamb chops! But how Christians are like sheep and Jesus is their Shepherd.

READ
John 10v11-13

WORD POOL
attack   die
knows   life   runs
sheep   wolf

Use the word pool words to fill in the gaps below.

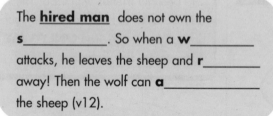

The **hired man** does not own the
s_____. So when a **w**_____
attacks, he leaves the sheep and **r**_____
away! Then the wolf can **a**_____
the sheep (v12).

The **Good Shepherd k**_____
his sheep well (v14). He lays down his
l_____ for the sheep (v11). He is ready
to **d**_____ for them!

Jesus is the
Good Shepherd!

READ
John 10v14-15

Jesus' followers (Christians) are like sheep. And Jesus is the good Shepherd who cares for them. To rescue His people from sin, Jesus was ready to **die** for them!

Turn to **God's Rescue Plan** on the next page to find out more.

THINK + PRAY

Jesus died to rescue anyone who trusts in Him! And we can get to know Jesus really really well. We can be close to Jesus, just as He is close to His Father, God. (v15) If you want to be Jesus' friend, tell Him right now.

GOD'S RESCUE PLAN

Jesus is the **Good Shepherd**. He cares for us and wants the best for us. He was prepared even to die for us to rescue us from **SIN**.

What is Sin?

It's not just wrong things. It's doing what **we** want instead of what **God** wants. The Bible says that all of us are like sheep, going our own way, instead of following Jesus, the **Good Shepherd**.

A lost sheep will die, because it has left the shepherd's care. We too will die, far away from God's love forever. A sheep can't find its shepherd. It needs to be rescued. So do we!

JESUS IS OUR RESCUER

But the great news is that Jesus came to **rescue** us from our sins!

How did Jesus rescue us?

At the first Easter, Jesus was nailed to a cross and left to die. As He died, Jesus rescued us from sin by taking all the punishment we deserve.

Did you know that God must punish the way we live? That's because we make His world bad and sad. But when He died, Jesus was punished instead of us, so we can be forgiven.

Did you know?

Jesus didn't stay dead! Three days later God brought Him back to life. Jesus is still alive today, looking after us and ruling as our **Shepherd King**.

I am the good shepherd. The good shepherd lays down his life for the sheep. (John 10v11)

When Jesus died He dealt with the problem of sin. That means that there is no longer any reason why we must be kept away from God's love and care.

Great news! Today God can be your Shepherd and King—and you can live in heaven with Him forever.

Have YOU been rescued by Jesus? Turn to the next page to find out more...

AM I A CHRISTIAN?

Not sure if you're a Christian? Then check it out below...

Christians are people who have been rescued by Jesus and follow Him as their Shepherd King.

> **You can't become a Christian by trying to be good.**

That's great news, since you can't be totally good all the time!

It's about accepting what Jesus did on the cross to rescue you. To do that, you will need to **ABCD**.

A **Admit** your sin—that you do, say and think wrong things. Tell God you are sorry. Ask Him to forgive you, and to help you to change. There will be some wrong things you have to stop doing.

B **Believe** that Jesus died for you, to take the punishment for your sin; that He came back to life, and that He is still alive today.

C **Consider** the cost of living like God's friend from now on, with Him in charge. It won't be easy. Ask God to help you do this.

D **Do** something about it! In the past you've gone your own way rather than God's way. Will you hand control of your life over to Him from now on? If you're ready to ABCD, then talk to God now. The prayer will help you.

A prayer

Dear God,
I have done and said and thought things that are wrong. I am really sorry. Please forgive me. Thank you for sending Jesus to die for me. From now on, please help me to live as one of Your friends, with You in charge.   Amen

> **Jesus welcomes <u>everyone</u> who comes to Him. If you have put your trust in Him, He has rescued you from your sins and will help you to live for Him. That's great news!**

Write down the names of people in your family.

READ
John 10v16

Jesus was talking to Jewish people. They were God's special people and thought they would be the **only ones** who would be with God in heaven.

*Use **verse 16** to fill in the missing first letters of words.*

I __ave __ther __heep that belong to me that are __ot of this __heep pen.

Jesus didn't come to rescue only Jewish people, but people from all backgrounds and parts of the world.

They shall be __ne __lock with one __hepherd (v16).

Jesus is the Good Shepherd who looks after His sheep, Christians. All Christians are in **one big family**, because they've all been **rescued by Jesus!**

READ
John 10v17-18

God loves Jesus because He <u>chose</u> to die for sinners like us. So God gave Jesus power, not only to give up His life to rescue us, but to come alive again and beat sin, death and the devil.

PRAY

Grab your XTB Writing Pad, and write down the names of Christians you know about in other countries. They're all part of God's big family! Pray for them, asking God to look after them and help them to serve Him.

DAY 23 FLOCK TACTICS

Some of the people want to know if Jesus really is the Christ —the King who God sent to rescue them (John 10v19-24).

READ
John 10v25-30

They had heard Jesus' amazing teaching and seen Him do awesome miracles. Yet they still wouldn't believe!

*Jesus promises three things for people who follow Him. Find them by taking the **first letter** of each picture.*

1. ___ ___ ___ ___ ___ ___

They are his friends! (v27)

2. ___ ___ ___ ___ ___ ___ ___ ___ ___ ___ ___ ___ ___ (v28)

They will live with Jesus for ever in heaven!

3. No one can

___ ___ ___ ___ ___ ___ ___ ___ (v29)

No one can take Christians away from Jesus!

Find another great fact from verse 30.

4. ___ ___ ___ ___ ___ ___

___ ___ ___ ___ ___ ___ ___ ___ ___

Jesus is God!
We can become friends with God!

PRAY

Read through boxes 1-4 again, thanking and praising Jesus for each great fact.

DAY 24 JESUS IS GOD!

Yesterday, we read that Jesus claimed to be **God**. So what did people think about that...

READ
John 10v31-33

Use the words in the box to fill in the gaps.

Jesus had shown these people many **m**_____. His power came from the **F**_____ (God). But the people wanted to **k**_____ Jesus. They said He was only a **m**_____ who was trying to make Himself **G**_____. (This was a very bad sin called blasphemy.)

God   does   kill   believe
miracles   Father   do   man

So if Jesus was only a man, He was also a very bad sinner.

But if Jesus was God, then the people who wouldn't believe in Him were sinners.

So, is Jesus really God or just a man?

This is the most important question you will ever have to answer! How can we find out the true answer?

READ
John 10v37-38

Jesus said...

Do not **b**_____ me unless I **d**___ what the Father (God) **d**_____.

Did Jesus do things that only God can do?   **Yes / No**

Should the people believe that Jesus was God?   **Yes / No**

Despite everything these people had seen and heard, they still **wouldn't** believe that Jesus was God! So Jesus went where people **would** believe Him. (v39-42)

PRAY

Do **YOU** believe that Jesus is God? Ask God to help you really trust that Jesus is God.

So that the Son of G_____ will be glorified through it.

Somehow, Lazarus being ill would lead people to see that Jesus is God's Son.

READ
John 11v11-16

Lazarus died! But Jesus was going to do something amazing. Why? Fill in the missing **a**s and **e**s please!

So th__t you m__y b__li__v__ . (v15)

READ
John 11v1-4

Mary, Martha and Lazarus were friends of Jesus. When Lazarus became very sick, they sent a message asking Jesus to help them.

 THINK SPOT — When something goes wrong in your life, is **Jesus** the first person you ask to help you?

What did Jesus say was the reason for Lazarus being ill (v4)?

READ
John 11v5-10

Jesus waited for _____ days before going to help Lazarus. It was dangerous to go because people wanted to

_____.

It seemed crazy to wait and even crazier to go. But Jesus knew what He was doing.

 THINK SPOT — When something goes wrong and God doesn't seem to help, can you still trust Him?

 **PRAY** — Jesus wanted His disciples to believe that He was God's Son. God is also working to make **you** think about turning to Jesus. Talk to God about this.

Jesus' friend Lazarus was really sick. But by the time Jesus arrived, Lazarus was already dead.

READ
John 11v17-22

Martha had wanted Jesus to heal Lazarus before he died. *Yet what did she say (v22)?* **Go forward one letter** *to find out (Z=A, A=B, B=C, C=D etc).*

F N C   V H K K   F H U D

X N T   V G Z S D U D Q

X N T   Z R J

Martha believed that Jesus could bring Lazarus back to life.

READ
John 11v23-26

Jesus said an incredible thing to Martha! *To find out what He means, fill in the gaps with the words* **LIFE, LIVE, DEATH** *and* **DIE**.

Jesus is the resurrection and the L_____ . Whoever turns to Him, will L_____ with Him for ever! Even though they will D_____, Jesus rescues them from D_____ in hell. They will L_____ with Jesus in heaven.

Read through the above box again. If you don't fully understand it, please ask an older Christian what it means!

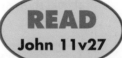

READ
John 11v27

Martha realised that Jesus was **the Christ**—the King who God sent to rescue us!

PRAY Thank you Jesus that You are the Christ and can rescue me so that I can live forever. Amen

Mary and Martha are Lazarus' sisters. Martha has already gone to meet Jesus. Now it's Mary's turn.

READ
John 11v28-31

THINK SPOT

When Mary heard that Jesus was there she rushed to meet Him. Are **YOU** excited about Jesus? Do you love to spend time talking to Him?

READ
John 11v32-35

When Jesus saw how upset Mary was, what did He do? **Cross out all the Xs** and write down the letters that are left.

XXXXJXXXXEXXXSX
XXUXXSXXXXWXXE
XXXPXXXXTXXXXX

J_____

Wow! Jesus is the Life. He <u>knew</u> Lazarus would be O.K. But He still wept! Death is our greatest enemy and Jesus knows and cares for how we feel—even though He's defeated death.

Jesus is a great example to us. He showed sympathy to Mary, and we should show sympathy to people who are sad.

Grab your **XTB Writing Pad**. Write down the names of people you know who are sad. Now write down ways you can show sympathy and friendship to them.

READ
John 11v36-37

Some people thought that Jesus couldn't bring Lazarus back to life. Tomorrow we'll see if Jesus could...

PRAY

Look at your writing pad. Ask God to comfort the people you've written down. Ask Him to help you show sympathy and friendship to them.

DAY 28 LIFE SAVER

READ
John 11v38-39

Lazarus had been dead for four days and his body was starting to smell! Yuck! But Jesus was about to do something incredible...

Jesus brought Lazarus back to life! Jesus has power over death! But why did Jesus do this amazing miracle?

READ
John 11v40-44

| S S O O T T H H A E T Y Y |
| B O E U L W I O E U V L E |
| D D S G E O E D G S O E D |
| N S T G J L E O S R U Y S |

To find the first reason, ***take every second letter*** *starting with the* ***first S***.

1. S_____
_____ (v40)
Jesus wants everyone to see how great God is!

xtb John 11v38-44

Now take every second letter starting with the **second S**.

2. S_____
_____
_____ (v42)
Jesus wants people to believe that God sent Him to earth to **rescue us from our sins**!

You've read all about Jesus and the amazing things He did. Do **YOU** believe that God sent Him to rescue you from your sinful ways? Not sure? Then turn to **God's Rescue Plan**, on the page after Day 21.

PRAY
Thank God that all Jesus' followers will come alive again in heaven—with better bodies than Lazarus and forever!

DAY 29 PERFECT PLAN!

Jesus brought Lazarus back to life to show that He was God's Son. Some people believed Him (John 11v45). But the Jewish leaders were worried that Jesus would become hugely popular and that the Romans might even destroy the Jewish nation! (verses 47-48)

READ
John 11v49-54

What did Caiaphas say? Start in the blue square and follow the maze, writing down the letters you pass.

I	D	E	D	E	T	A	N
T	I	O	Y	E	B	I	L	E
B	S	R	T	S	N	O	O	H
E	F	O	R	O	I	E	T	W
T	R	M	E	N	D	A	H	E
T	E	A	N	T	O	N	T	H

It is _____

_____

_____ (v50)

What Caiaphas said has two very different meanings!

Caiaphas meant that they should kill Jesus to <u>SAVE</u> the Jews from being destroyed by the Romans.

Jesus' death would <u>SAVE</u> people. But not from the Romans! It would save people from being punished for their sins!

And not just Jewish people. God used this **wicked plot** to carry out His **wonderful plan** to rescue people!

PRAY

Thank you God for Your brilliant rescue plan. Thank you that if I ask Jesus to, He will forgive my sins. Amen

John 12v1-11

Jesus went back to visit Lazarus and his sisters, Mary and Martha. After hearing about Jesus bringing Lazarus back to life, many people **believed Jesus was God's Son**. So the evil Jewish leaders wanted to kill Lazarus as well as Jesus (it's in John 12v9-11).

READ
John 12v1-3

*Show what Mary did for Jesus by filling in all the missing **e**'s.*

Mary pour__d v__ry __xp__nsiv__ p__rfum__ on J__sus' f__ __t and wip__d his f__ __t with h__r hair.

Only slaves would usually wash dusty, stinky feet. And not with their hair! But Mary loved Jesus so much that she washed Jesus' dusty feet using very expensive perfume!

In your XTB Writing Pad, write <u>WHAT I CAN DO FOR JESUS</u> at the top of a page. Now list some things you can do to show how much you love Jesus (eg: talking to Him more, helping round the home, telling friends about Him).

READ
John 12v4-8

Judas complained about Mary using such expensive perfume on Jesus. If you do things for Jesus you can expect people to hassle you unfairly.

But Jesus knew that He would soon die and that Mary had done a lovely thing for Him before He died.

PRAY How much do you love Jesus? Ask God to help you do the things you have written down. Now do them!

READ
John 12v12-13

The people of Jerusalem all shouted and cheered for Jesus! *What did they call Him (v13)? Use the flag code.*

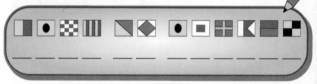

Jesus was the King sent by God to **rescue** the people of Israel. But they thought He should be a mighty warrior who would bash the Romans. They were wrong.

READ
John 12v14-19

Instead of a warhorse, Jesus rode on a young donkey! Just as the prophet Zechariah had said 500 years earlier! (It's in Zechariah 9v9-11.)

Flag Code

Flag	=
	= A
	= B
	= C
	= E
	= F
	= G
	= H
●	= I
	= K
	= L
	= N
	= O
	= P
	= R
	= S
	= T
	= U

Find three things Zechariah said Jesus would do.

1. _____

2. _____

3. _____

_____

Jesus died on the cross to **bring peace** to the world and to free people who are **prisoners to sin**. One day He will rule everyone everywhere!

PRAY Thank God that people were wrong, but Zechariah was right, about King Jesus.

Jesus will teach us four **top truths** today! Read the Bible bits in **BLUE** and fill in the missing vowels (aeiou).

TOP TRUTH 1
Read John 12v20-22

These Greek guys show us that Jesus didn't just come for Jewish people, but Gentiles (non-Jews) too. **Anyone can turn to Jesus to have their sins forgiven!**

J___s___s came for the whole w___rld!

TOP TRUTH 2
Read John 12v23-24

A seed must fall from a plant and **die** before a new plant can grow from it. Jesus knew that He would soon **die**. But His death would bring everlasting **life** to anyone who turns to Him for forgiveness.

Jesus' d___ ___th gives l___fe!

TOP TRUTH 3
Read John 12v25

People who live to please themselves instead of God will be punished. But people who **put God first** will live with Him for ever!

We must love G___d, not lif___

TOP TRUTH 4
Read John 12v26

If you're serious about following Jesus, then you've got to **show it in the way you live your life**. It pleases God when we do.

We must s___rve Jesus

Two days ago, you wrote down **WHAT I CAN DO FOR JESUS** in your writing pad. Have you done any of those things? Will you try to do them?

PRAY　Read Top Truths 1 and 2. Thank God for them! Now read Top Truths 3 and 4. Ask God to help you do those things.

DAY 33 WHY DID JESUS DIE?

John 12v27-36

Jesus explained why He had to die.

READ
John 12v27-33

It's very hard to understand isn't it? Jesus said that the whole purpose of Him coming to earth was to **die!**

Find four amazing things that Jesus' death would do. **Go forward one letter** *(Z=A, A=B, B=C, C=D etc).*

1. _ _ _ _   _ _ _ _ _
   F H U D   F K N Q X
   _ _   _ _ _ (v28)
   S N   F N C

People would see how **great and loving** God is. He sent His own Son to rescue them!

2. _ _ _ _ _   _ _ _
   I T C F D   S G D
   _ _ _ _ _ (v31)
   V N Q K C

People who turn to Jesus for forgiveness will be **rescued** from sin. Those who don't will be **punished** by God. (*That's what verses 34-36 are all about.*)

3. _ _ _ _   _ _ _
   A D Z S   S G D
   _ _ _ _ _ (v31)
   C D U H K

When Jesus died and was raised back to life, the devil was defeated!

4. _ _ _ _   _ _ _
   C Q Z V   Z K K
   _ _ _ _ _   _ _
   O D N O K D   S N
   _ _ _ _ _ (v32)
   I D R T R

Jesus' death made it possible for **anyone** to be forgiven and become Jesus' friends.

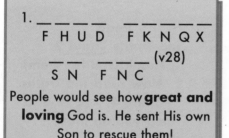

For the free e-booklet **Why did Jesus die?** email alison@thegoodbook.co.uk

PRAY Read through the four boxes again. Now talk to God and tell Him exactly how you feel.

DAY 34 LIGHTEN UP!

Many people saw Jesus' miracles, like bringing Lazarus back to life. It all happened just as God's messenger Isaiah had said, 700 years earlier! (John 12v37-41) **But** they still wouldn't believe that Jesus was God's Son.

READ
John 12v42-43

Loads of people **did** believe Jesus! *But what was the problem?*

They were scared of the Pharisees ☐

They wanted men to praise them ☐

They didn't care enough about God ☐

They're all true!

They wanted to believe in Jesus **secretly**, without anyone knowing.

> Great idea! You can be a Christian but your friends won't laugh at you!

BUT what does Jesus say?

READ
John 12v44-46

Fill in the gaps.

v44

If you **b**_____ in me, you will also **b**_____ in the one who **s**_____ me (God).

That means nothing is more important than God—not even friends!

v46

I have come into the **w**_____ as a **L**_____. If you **b**_____ in me you won't stay in **d**_____.

Everyone lives in darkness because they disobey God. But a Christian follows Jesus the light, so they live differently. You can't do it secretly!

THINK SPOT

Do your friends know that you believe in Jesus? Perhaps they laugh about it and make it hard for you? But are you more bothered about what people think? Or about what God thinks of you?

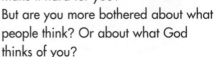

Don't forget that Jesus also said that, in the end, God will punish everyone who doesn't believe in Jesus. (v47-50)

PRAY

Ask God to help you live Jesus' way boldly (not secretly) and to turn your back on the wrong things you do, even if others laugh at you.

 John 13v1-17

Jesus knew that He would soon be betrayed by Judas and would die and go back to heaven. Yet He still did a great thing for His friends...

READ
John 13v1-5

Jesus was God's Son, yet He got down and washed His friends' grubby feet!

READ
John 13v6-11

Jesus **washed** His disciples' feet as a picture of something more amazing. It was to show that Jesus **would wash their sins away**. He would forgive them for all the sins they had done. And He'll do the same for us if we ask Him!

What did Jesus say when He washed Simon Peter's feet? *Discover it by crossing out **every third letter** and writing out the ones you're left with.*

YOTUHHAVEEASLREEAL
DYEBETENTWAESHREDSFRS
OMHYOOURUSILNSDYOB
UOENLCYNREEODYSOUS
RFEEEDTWOASUHITNG

Y_ _ _   _ _ _ _ _

_ _ _ _ _ _ _ _ _

_ _ _ _   _ _ _ _ _ . Y _ _

_ _ _ _ _ _ _

_ _ _ _ _ _ _ .

Being washed all over is a picture of being forgiven for **all** the wrong things we'll ever do. That happens when we believe in Jesus.

Having our feet washed is a picture of saying sorry to God **each time** we do wrong. And remembering that, through Jesus, we've been forgiven.

READ
John 13v12-17

Like Jesus, we should serve others. In your **XTB Writing Pad** write down some names. Next to them write down how you can **serve** them this week (polish shoes, be nicer to them etc). Don't write down stuff you already do!

PRAY

Dear God, thank you for sending Jesus to wash our sins away. Please help me do what I've written and be like Jesus.

DAY 36 · HISTORY HOP

A quick pogo through the history of the Israelites...

THREE PROMISES

God made three amazing promises to **Abraham**.

1 **A HUGE family**.

◼◻🔲◀◼◼⬤◼◻◼◻

The _ _ _ _ _ _ _ _ _ .

2 **A land of their own**.

⬤◼🔲◀◼◼

The land of _ _ _ _ _ _ .

3 **Blessing**. Someone from Abraham's family would be

🔲◥🔲◼◼

God's way of blessing the whole _ _ _ _ _ .

A= ◀ D= ◼ E= ◼ H= ◻

I= ⬤ L= ◼ M= ⊠

N= ▨ O= ◥ R= 🔲 S= ◻

T= ◻ V= ⊠ W= 🔲

The Israelites lived in Egypt for 400 years. They became a HUGE family (over two million!) *just as God had promised*.

But the Egyptians made them into _ _ _ _ _ _ !

So God rescued the Israelites from Egypt, and brought them to the land of Israel, *just as He had promised*.

For 400 years, the Israelites had a series of leaders called **judges**. After that they had **kings** to lead them.

◼◀⊠⬤◼

The best king they ever had was _ _ _ _ _ .
David loved God, and helped his people to love God too.

A WARNING ◼◥◼◥⊠◼▨

When David died, his son _ _ _ _ _ _ _ became king. God told Solomon what would happen if he and his family loved and <u>obeyed</u> God. He also told Solomon what would happen if he <u>disobeyed</u> God...

Turn to the next page to find out more.

READ
1 Kings 9v4-9

If Solomon and his family <u>loved</u> and <u>obeyed</u> God, someone from their family would always rule the Israelites (v4-5).

> But what would happen if they <u>turned away</u> from God, and served pretend gods (idols) instead? (v7)
>
> **a)** God would remove them from the land of Israel
> **b)** God would ignore them
> **c)** God would give them more land

Did you know?

This was a serious warning, which God gave the Israelites many times. It was **God** who had given them the land of Israel to live in. But if they kept turning away from Him, He would <u>remove</u> them from that land.

In the next chunk of 2 Kings, we'll see God's warning come true. It's a sad story, as we see the Israelites <u>turned out</u> of their land because they <u>turned away</u> from God.

> ● ■ ◀ ● ◀ ▯
>
> But we'll also meet a chap called __ __ __ __ __ __.

Isaiah has some exciting things to say about God's promise, that someone from Abraham's family will be God's way of **blessing the whole world**!

PRAY

History = <u>His</u> Story.
The history of the Israelites teaches us loads about what <u>God</u> is like and how He acts. Ask Him to help you learn more about Him as you read this part of Israel's history.

DAY 37 SPOT THE KINGS

The Israelites were split into two kingdoms. They were called **Israel** (in the north) and **Judah** (in the south).

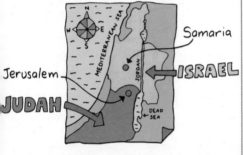

Today's sad story is about the kingdom of **Israel**, and its very <u>last</u> king.

*As you read the story, draw a **crown** in the box every time you read the name of another king.*

READ
2 Kings 17v1-6

The four kings were:
- **Ahaz**—king of Judah
- **Hoshea**—king of Israel
- **Shalmaneser**—king of Assyria
- **So**—king of Egypt

Fill in the correct letters in each crown. The first one is done for you.

[crown] was king of Israel for nine years. Every year [crown] payed money to [crown] the king of Assyria. But one year, [crown] sent messengers to [crown] the king of Egypt asking for help against the Assyrians. When [crown] the king of Assyria found out, he had [crown] thrown into prison. Then [crown] the king of Assyria attacked the city of Samaria. [crown] captured the Israelites and sent them away to Assyria.

There are lots of kings in today's story. But there's one missing! Who do you think it is? Think carefully, then use yesterday's code to check your answer.

___ ___ ___   ___ ___ ___ ___

God had warned the Israelites that He would remove them from their land if they turned away from Him. So when the king of Assyria captured the Israelites and sent them to Assyria, he was doing what <u>God</u> had said would happen. God was in control all the time—**He** is the REAL KING!

PRAY

God is far more powerful than any king, president or prime minister! Talk to Him about how that makes you feel.

DAY 38 KICKED OUT!

The Israelites had been kicked out of Israel, and sent away to Assyria. The next few verses tell us **why**...

READ
2 Kings 17v7-8

Why were the Israelites kicked out of their land? (v7)

> They had **s**_____ against the **L**_____ their **G**_____.

Take the first letter of each pic to see some of the things the Israelites did.

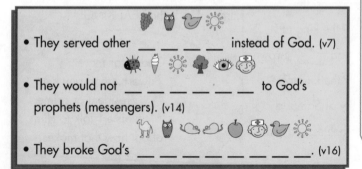

- They served other ___ ___ ___ instead of God. (v7)

- They would not ___ ___ ___ ___ to God's prophets (messengers). (v14)

- They broke God's ___ ___ ___ ___ ___ ___ ___ ___. (v16)

In the past, Israel had an evil king called Jeroboam. He had led the Israelites to abandon God and break His laws. For 400 years they had carried on living that way...

READ
2 Kings 17v22-23

How did God punish them? (v23)

They were taken into 👁 🩻 🍦 🐞 👁

___ ___ ___ ___ ___.

> ### Did you know?
> **Exile** means being kicked out of your home and country —and never being allowed to return.

God had done **so much** for the Israelites. He had <u>rescued</u> them from Egypt (v7), brought them to the <u>land</u> He promised, and sent many <u>prophets</u> to tell them God's words (v13). But the Israelites turned away from God, and ignored His words.

THINK + PRAY

What about you? God has done **so much** for <u>you</u> too. Is there anything you need to say sorry to Him for? Think carefully, and then talk to God about it.

DAY 39 MEET THE SAMARITANS

Do you know who the Samaritans are?
a) A charity that helps people.
b) A group of people who lived at the time of Jesus.
c) A group we will meet in 2 Kings.

Check your answer at the bottom of the page.

Did you know?

When the king of Assyria captured the Israelites and sent them to live in Assyria, he needed to put some other people in their place. They would look after the land and pay him taxes. The people he moved in became known as the **Samaritans** (because they lived in **Samaria**).

READ
2 Kings 17v24-28

The people who lived in Samaria didn't worship God. What did He do? (v25)

**He sent
l_____!**

The king of Assyria heard that God had sent lions because the people in Samaria didn't worship Him. Who did the king send to Samaria? (v27)

A p_____

The priest taught the people how to love and serve God.

BUT the people served <u>other</u> gods (idols) as well as God! (v29-41)

God hates sin. He hates it if people make something else more important than Him. The people living in Samaria didn't love and serve God —so He sent lions to punish them.

THINK SPOT

Every time you and I make something else more important than God—or we fail to love and serve God totally—then we are **sinning**. And that sin must be punished.

But the great news is that God has made a way for us to be forgiven! *Copy the red letters (in order) to see what that way is.*

_ _ _ _ _ _ _

_ _ _ _ _ _

To find out more, check out 'God's Rescue Plan' after Day 21.

PRAY

God sent Jesus, not a punishment! Are you thankful? Then say so!

DAY 40 THE GOOD SAMARITAN

 xtb Luke 10v25-37

Who were the group of people we met yesterday?

The S_____

Does that name ring any bells? Today we're going to hop into the New Testament to read a story Jesus told...

READ
Luke 10v25-28

An expert in Old Testament law asked Jesus a question about eternal life. He wanted to know how to <u>earn</u> a place in heaven.

*Use a **mirror** to read the answer.*

- **Love** God with all your **ʇɹɐǝɥ** and **lnoƨ** and **ɥʇƃuǝɹʇƨ** and **bnim**.
- **Love** your **ɹnoqɥƃıǝu** as yourself.

That means:
- Love God totally—all the time.
- Love other people—all the time.

Can you do that? <u>ALL</u> the time???

Yes / No

The answer is No! So we can't <u>earn</u> our place in heaven. That's why Jesus came and died for us. **He** is the only way we can be forgiven, and one day live with God in heaven.

But the law expert had another tricky question:

 Who is my neighbour?

He wanted to know exactly <u>who</u> he had to love. So Jesus told him a story. The main characters are:
- A Jewish man (*who gets beaten up*)
- A priest (*chosen to serve God*)
- A Levite (*a helper in God's temple*)
- A Samaritan (*<u>hated</u> by the Jews*)

READ
Luke 10v29-37

Who was a neighbour (friend) to the injured man?
- **a)** The priest
- **b)** The Levite
- **c)** The Samaritan

Jesus told the law expert to go and do the same. In other words, he had to love his <u>enemies</u> as well as his friends!

THINK+PRAY

Love God totally and love other people.

If we are Christians (followers of Jesus), then this is how we will want to live. <u>Not</u> to earn a place in heaven! But because we want to <u>please</u> God by living His way. Ask God to help you to do this today... and tomorrow... and the day after... and...

- The people in Israel had been taken away by the Assyrians. 😕
- God had warned them that this would happen if they kept sinning, but they ignored His warnings. 🙁
- The people who moved in (the Samaritans) weren't any better. They learnt to worship God, but served other gods too! 😕

🙁 **All very dismal**.

Ready for some good news?? 🙂 All of this happened in the northern kingdom of Israel. But in the southern kingdom of Judah there was a new king. His name was **Hezekiah** (we'll call him Hez!), and Hez loved and obeyed God. **Yippee!!** 🙂

READ
2 Kings 18v1-8

Hez did what was **right** in God's eyes, as King **David** had. He **destroyed** everything that had been used to worship pretend gods. Hez **trusted** God. None of the other **kings** of Judah were like him. Hez was faithful to God and **kept** all of His commands. **God** was **with** Hez, and gave him success in everything he did.

Fit the blue words into the puzzle. The yellow boxes will spell two new words.

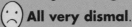

THINK SPOT

Hez trusted God (v5). Trusting God isn't just about what we believe. It's also about what we do. Hez did all these things because he trusted God, and believed that obeying God's commands is the best way to live. 🙂

THINK + PRAY

What about you? If you trust God, you'll want to obey His commands, even when that's hard. Firstly that means:
- Believing in Jesus
  Then you can please God by:
- Always telling the truth.
- Loving other people.
- Obeying your parents.
- Telling others about Jesus.
Ask God to help you trust Him by doing these things.

DAY 42 WHO DO YOU TRUST?

xtb 2 Kings 18v17-25

On Day 38 we saw how Shalmaneser, King of Assyria, captured the city of Samaria. Now the next king of Assyria, called Sennacherib, wanted to do the same to Jerusalem!

He sent a message to King Hezekiah in Jerusalem.

On what are you basing your trust?

What do you think Hezekiah's answer would be? What or who did he trust?

Check your answer in yesterday's puzzle.

Sennacherib tried to knock Hezekiah's trust in God...

READ
2 Kings 18v19-25

⇨ = A ⇦ = B ⇔ = D ⇗ = E → = G

↑ = H ↙ = L ↘ = M ↕ = O

▲ = P △ = R ▽ = S ◀ = T ◢ = Y

⇨ → ◢ ▲ ▲ ◀
- _ _ _ _ _ _ won't help you.
  (v21)

→ ↕ ⇦
- _ _ _ won't help you.
  (v22)

⇨ △ ↘ ◢
- Your _ _ _ _ can't help you.
  (v24)

→ ↕ ⇦
- It was _ _ _ who told us to attack you!
  (v25)

Sennacherib was trying to make Hezekiah and the Israelites lose their confidence in God. Would it work?

More tomorrow...

You don't believe all that rubbish in the Bible do you???

Nobody believes in Jesus any more!

THINK + PRAY

Do you ever get teased for being a Christian? It can be really tough sometimes. Ask God to help you to hold on to the truth from the Bible:
—that God is the Real King of everything;
—that God loves you;
—that God sent His own Son to die for you, so that you can be forgiven and one day live with Him in heaven.

DAY 43 ⇦ ↙ ⇨ ▽ ▲ ↑ ⇨ ↘ ▲

Use yesterday's code to discover today's heading.

What is blasphemy?
a) talking too much
b) saying things against God
c) singing too loudly

King Sennacherib of Assyria has sent his messenger to Jerusalem. He is saying stuff against God—that's blasphemy! And the messenger is deliberately speaking in the common language of Hebrew so that the Israelites crowded onto the walls of Jerusalem can all understand him...

READ
2 Kings 18v26-37

What was Sennacherib's message?

LORD   save   trust   gods

Don't let Hezekiah persuade you to
t_____ in the LORD. (v30)

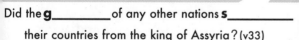

Did the **g**_____ of any other nations **s**_____
their countries from the king of Assyria? (v33)

How then can the **L**_____ save Jerusalem? (v35)

The message is clear. The king of Assyria thinks he is far more powerful than any god. Not even the LORD can stop him! That's **blasphemy**! And he's very wrong, as we'll see tomorrow...

THINK SPOT

Hopefully <u>you</u> never say stuff against God the way Sennacherib did! But do you ever use God's name carelessly? *Fill in the gaps to see some examples.*

wrong
name
swear
joke

Never
j_____
about God.

And don't think
w_____
things about God.

And don't use God's
n_____ (or 'Jesus')
as a **s**_____ word.

THINK + PRAY

Do you ever use God's name as a swear word? Or think wrong things about God? If you do, tell Him you are sorry, and ask Him to help you to change.

DAY 44 DON'T BE AFRAID!

xtb 2 Kings 19v1-7

What do you wear at church?

Draw or write your answer.

Before going to the temple, King Hezekiah ripped his clothes and put on sackcloth! *Read the verses to see why.*

READ
2 Kings 19v1-4

Did you know?

In Bible times, people tore their clothes and wore sackcloth when they were terribly sad or upset. Hezekiah was upset because the king of Assyria had threatened Jerusalem and insulted God.

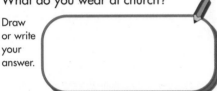

Hezekiah sent his men to see God's prophet (messenger). What was he called? (v2)

I_____

Isaiah had a message for Hezekiah. It was a message from **God**...

return
king
Don't
die

READ
2 Kings 19v5-7

D_____ be afraid. (v6)
The **k**_____ of Assyria will hear a report that will make him
r_____ to his country. I will cause him to **d**_____ there. (v7)

Did you know?

The most often repeated command in the Bible is 'Don't be afraid'. It's repeated 366 times. That's one for each day of the year, and one extra in case you have a particularly scary day!

God told Hezekiah not to be afraid. Why? Because **God** is the Real King. He's far more powerful than the king of Assyria!

THINK + PRAY

We have the same reason not to be afraid. God is the Real King today too. He is always able to help us, and never lets us down. So talk to Him about your worries—and ask Him to help you not to be afraid.

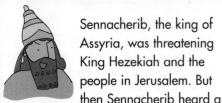

Sennacherib, the king of Assyria, was threatening King Hezekiah and the people in Jerusalem. But then Sennacherib heard a report that another king was attacking him!—just as **God** had said he would.

But Sennacherib tried again to make Hezekiah stop trusting God. This time he wrote a letter saying that <u>no</u> god could stop the Assyrians! (v8-13)

When Hezekiah received the letter, he went to the temple to talk to God.

READ
2 Kings 19v14-19

O Lord, you **alone** are God over all the kingdoms of the **earth**. **Hear**, LORD, and **listen**. Open your eyes, LORD, and **see**. Listen to what **Sennacherib** has said to insult the **living** God. **Save** us from his power, so that all the **kingdoms** on earth will know that you, O **LORD**, are the only God.

Find all of the <u>blue</u> words in the wordsearch. (Some are backwards!)

Y	L	I	V	I	N	G	R	A	E	H
O	U	E	N	O	L	A	S	A	V	E
O	L	O	K	I	N	G	D	O	M	S
S	E	N	N	A	C	H	E	R	I	B
E	A	R	T	H	R	D	A	R	E	T
N	E	T	S	I	L	H	E	O	N	L
L	O	R	D	E	E	S	Y	G	O	D

Copy the leftover letters from the wordsearch.

_ _ _ _   _ _ _ _ _ _

_ _ _   _ _ _ _ _

_ _ _ _ _ _   _ _ _ _

You can find the answer on your XTB Writing Pad!

Hezekiah's prayer is a great example for us to follow:
1. He praised God. (v15)
2. He told God the problem. (v16-18)
3. He asked God to act in a way that would show how great God is. (v19)

PRAY

Use your XTB Writing Pad to write your <u>own</u> prayer to God, following Hezekiah's pattern of **1,2,3**.

DAY 46 A HOOK IN YOUR NOSE!

King Hezekiah has been praying in the temple—asking God to save Jerusalem from the Assyrians. Now he gets an answer from God—sent by God's messenger, Isaiah.

READ
2 Kings 19v20-28

The first part of God's message was to Sennacherib, the king of Assyria. *Take the first letter of each pic to see what it is.*

- Jerusalem __ __ __ __ __ __ at you Sennacherib. (v21)

- Who do you think you've been __ __ __ __ __ __ __ __ __ __ ? (v22)

- You have used your messengers to insult the __ __ __ __ . (v23)

- Long ago I, the LORD, __ __ __ __ __ __ __ these things. I allowed you to turn these strong walled cities into piles of rock. (v25)

- I have heard of your pride. So I will put my __ __ __ __ in your nose and my bit in your mouth. Then I will force you to return by the way you came. (v28)

Did you know?

A farmer leads a bull by a **ring** or **hook** in its nose. A rider uses a **bit** to tell his horse where to go. In the same way, God would force Sennacherib to leave Jerusalem and return to Assyria.

We'll see how God did that tomorrow.

PRAY

God's enemies (*those who hate Christians, the devil*) have to do what <u>God</u> wants. Eg: when God's enemies killed Jesus they carried out <u>God's</u> plan to rescue us! Thank God that He is always in control.

DAY 47 **THE HOOK WORKS!**

God had said:
• The king of Assyria will return to his own country, and I will cause him to be killed there. (v7)
• I will put my hook in his nose, and my bit in his mouth, and force him to return the way he came.

God then promised Hezekiah that Jerusalem and the land around it would recover from being attacked (v29-31) and that the king of Assyria would never enter it (v32-34).

 THINK SPOT
Do you think God's words came true?

Yes / No
Not sure

Why do you think that?

Now read the passage to find out.

READ
2 Kings 19v35-37

 Who went to the Assyrian camp? (v35)

The **a**_____ of the **L**_____

How many Assyrians were killed? (v35)

165,000   **175,000**   **185,000**

God said the king of Assyria would return home (to Assyria, and its capital city Nineveh). Did he? (v36)   **Yes / No**

God said the king of Assyria would be killed in Assyria. Was he? (v37)   **Yes / No**

PRAY
God's words <u>always</u> come true. Why?
—because God always speaks the **truth**!
—because God is always **able** to do what He says!
—because nothing and no one can **stop** God's plans!
Thank and praise God for these things.

PS: God **rescued** His people, just as He promised. Can you think of another way God rescues His people? *More about that on Day 55.*

King Hezekiah became ill. <u>Very</u> ill. In fact, he was going to die!

READ
2 Kings 20v1-3

What did Hezekiah do?

• He **p**_____ (v2)

• He _____ bitterly (v3)

THINK SPOT

When you're ill, or upset, do you pray about it? You can talk to God about <u>anything</u> —and it's OK to show Him how upset you are, too!

God heard Hezekiah's prayer, and sent Isaiah back with another message...

READ
2 Kings 20v4-7

What was God's message? (v5)

> I have **h**_____ your
> prayer and **s**_____ your
> tears. I will **h**_____ you.

Instead of dying, Hezekiah was going to live another _____ years! (v6)

That was great news! But Hezekiah wanted a **sign** that it would really happen just as God said...

READ
2 Kings 20v8-11

Hmm... Nobody's quite sure what this sign was. It may have been a special staircase that used a <u>shadow</u> to tell the time (a bit like a sundial). Whatever it was, we **do** know that God generously gave Hezekiah the sign he asked for (v11).

THINK SPOT

Praying for people who are ill can feel a bit puzzling. Sometimes God heals them quickly (like Hezekiah). Sometimes He heals them slowly, and uses doctors and nurses to make them better. And sometimes they may not get better at all. That doesn't mean God hasn't heard our prayers! But He may have a good reason for saying No.

Do you remember reading about the blind man, and Jesus' friend Lazarus, in John's Gospel? These men were ill so that God's work could be seen in their lives. (*Flick back to Days 16 and 25 if you don't remember these stories.*)

PRAY

Pray for anyone you know who is ill. Ask God to be with them, and to do what He knows is best for them.

DAY 49 VISITORS FROM BABYLON

FLASHBACK *(Cross out the **X**'s)*

• The Israelites were split into two kingdoms, called **XXIXSRXAXELXX** and **XJXXUDXXAXHXX**.

• The people in <u>Israel</u> had been taken away by the **XASXSYXRIXAXNSX**.

• God had <u>warned</u> them that this would happen if they kept on sinning, but they **XIXGNXXORXEXXDXX** Him!

Hezekiah, the king of **Judah**, was a good king who loved and obeyed God. But God had made the same warning to the people of Judah. If they <u>turned away</u> from God, they would be <u>turned out</u> of their country!

READ
2 Kings 20v12-15

Where were the messengers from? (v12)
- **a)** Birmingham
- **b)** Babylon
- **c)** Brisbane

What did Hezekiah show them? (v15)
- **a)** Nothing
- **b)** Everything
- **c)** His pet hamster

Then **Isaiah** turned up with a message from God...

READ
2 Kings 20v16-21

What was God's message? (v17)

The **t**_____ will come when **e**_____ in your palace will be **c**_____ off to **B**_____.

It wouldn't happen while Hezekiah was alive—but it <u>would</u> happen. The people of Judah would be taken away, just like the people of Israel. *More about that when we return to 2 Kings on Day 56.*

PRAY

Hezekiah had been a good king, like King David. But he wasn't perfect! God's <u>perfect</u> King, also from David's family, would be born 700 years later. Thank God for sending **King J**_____ to be our perfect King.

DAY 50 WHOLLY HOLY

We're going to jump out of **2 Kings** for a few days to find out how the prophet **Isaiah** got his job as God's messenger.

READ
Isaiah 6v1-4

Isaiah saw a great King, sitting on a throne. But it wasn't King Uzziah! Who was the King? (v1)

The L_____

How is God described? (v1)

Seated on a **t**_____.
H_____ and exalted.
His robe filled the **t**_____.

Wow! God is the King of the whole universe! No one is higher or more powerful than Him!

Word pool

high
holy
throne
holy
LORD
glory
holy
temple

The throne was surrounded by **seraphs**. These amazing creatures were like fiery angels. They <u>worshipped</u> God. What were they saying? (v3)

H_____, h_____, h_____ is the LORD Almighty! The whole earth is full of his g_____.

Wow! God it totally perfect and pure! He made the whole earth, and it shows how great and wonderful He is!

THINK + PRAY

Copy the seraph's words from verse 3 onto your XTB Writing Pad. Now turn that page into a paper aeroplane! Choose someone you would like to pray with, and fly the plane to them. (*If you're alone, pray by yourself for now and try to find someone to fly your plane with tomorrow.*) Ask them to undo it and read the verse aloud. Then pray together, praising God for being King of the universe, holy, perfect and pure.

DAY 51 UNCLEAN LIPS

Isaiah had just seen God, sitting on His throne as King of the universe, surrounded by fiery angels!

What do you think Isaiah thought?
- Wow! I'm so pleased I'm here!
- I wish I had a camera.
- I wonder what God wants.
- _____

Read the passage to find out.

READ
Isaiah 6v5-7

Code key:

A =
C =
E =
G =
I =
J =
K =
L =
N =
O =
S =
U =
W =

___ ___ ___ to me!

I am a man of ___ ___ ___ ___ ___ ___ ___ lips.

My eyes have seen the ___ ___ ___ ___ , the LORD Almighty.

Um??? What are 'unclean lips'? Did Isaiah have a muddy face?

XTB XPLANATION

Isaiah knew he was **sinful**. Even his <u>lips</u> spoke sinful words. But God is holy, perfect and pure. Isaiah knew that he didn't deserve to be with God. In fact, he deserved to die!

But God did something wonderful for Isaiah...

> One of the seraphs **f**_____ to Isaiah with a burning **c**_____ from the **a**_____. He touched Isaiah's **l**_____ with it, and Isaiah's **g**_____ was taken away and his **s**_____ forgiven!

God made Isaiah clean again! His sins were forgiven.

Who has made it possible for <u>our</u> sins to be forgiven?

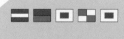
___ ___ ___ ___ ___

PRAY

Thank God for sending Jesus so that we can be made clean and have our sins forgiven. (*More about that on Day 55.*)

WHO WILL GO?

- Isaiah had <u>seen</u> God his King.
- And God had <u>forgiven</u> Isaiah's sin.

Now God had a question for Isaiah...

READ
Isaiah 6v8

Fill in the gaps.

Whom shall I s_____?

Send m_____!

A HARD MESSAGE

Isaiah had volunteered to be God's messenger. Now he needed to know what the message was...

READ
Isaiah 6v9-10

God's message to the Israelites was a tough one. *Cross out the **X**'s.*

Be **XHXEAXRIXNXGX** but never **XUNXDEXRSXTAXNXDIXNGX**.

God's people had turned away from Him. So now they wouldn't <u>understand</u> God's message to them.

A HINT OF GOOD NEWS TO COME

For how long, O LORD?

The land God had given His people would be ruined. But there was still a <u>hint</u> of a hope to come...

READ
Isaiah 6v11-13

New trees can grow from bare stumps. In the same way there was still a <u>hope</u> for the people of Judah. Out of the very few who accepted God, His people would grow again. And one of them would be the perfect King they were waiting for! *More about Him tomorrow...*

THINK + PRAY

Read v8 again. Isaiah offered to serve God straight away. Have <u>you</u> ever told God that you want to serve Him? Don't think that you're too young! If you want to serve God with your life, then ask Him to show you how He wants you to do that. Talk to Him about it now.

DAY 53 TO US A CHILD IS BORN

Isaiah had a hard message for the Israelites. But there were some fantastic clues about the perfect King who God had promised to send...

READ
Isaiah 9v1-2

The people walking in **d**_____ have seen a great **l**_____.

Where would this great light be seen? (v1) **G**_____

Did you know?

Jesus grew up in Nazareth, which is in <u>Galilee</u>. **Jesus** is the 'great light' Isaiah was speaking about!

Isaiah went on to say that God's people would have **peace** when their perfect King came.

READ
Isaiah 9v6-7

You may have heard these words at a Christmas Carol Service. *Fill in some of the fantastic names for Jesus.*

W_____ **Counsellor**

M_____ **God**

Everlasting F_____

P_____ **of Peace**

Jesus shows us the best way to live, and brings us <u>peace</u> with God. Jesus <u>is</u> God! He is mighty and everlasting!

How long will Jesus be King? (v7)
a) a short time
b) a hundred years
c) for ever

PRAY

Wow! Jesus is our perfect King! He is still alive today—and will rule as King for ever! Thank, praise and obey Him right now.

Take the first letter of each pic to see some of the ways Isaiah has described Jesus.

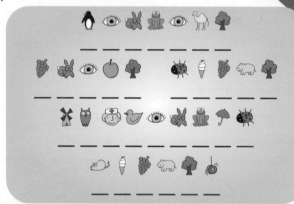

Wow! Jesus is fantastic! Surely everyone would be <u>thrilled</u> when this perfect King arrived... But they weren't!

Here's another way that Isaiah described Jesus:

Isaiah 52v13–53v12 was written hundreds of years before Jesus was born. But it describes how people would <u>hate</u> Jesus and turn their backs on Him, even though He had come as their perfect King.

READ
Isaiah 53v3

- **Despised**: People looked down on Jesus.
- **Rejected**: People turned away from Jesus.
- **Suffering**: Jesus died a horrible, painful death.

WHY did Jesus go through all of this?

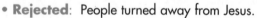

To _ _ _ _ _ _ _ us from our _ _ _ _.

More about this tomorrow.

PRAY Thank Jesus for being willing to be despised and rejected, and to suffer so much, to be our Rescuer and King.

DAY 55 WE'RE ALL LIKE SHEEP...

Ahem! The book of Isaiah has some tricky terms in it. Just in case—here are a few you might meet today.

Sins/Infirmities/ Transgressions/Iniquities
All of these words are used for our **sin**, when we do what <u>we</u> want instead of what <u>God</u> wants.

Stricken/Smitten/Afflicted
These words mean that Jesus was made to <u>suffer</u>.

As you read today's verses, remember that Jesus <u>chose</u> to suffer, so that He could be our Rescuer.

READ
Isaiah 53v4-6

Fill in the gaps to see the **XTB Xplanation** of verse 6.

Jesus own God sheep

• We are all like **s**_____ who have wandered off and got lost.

• We've gone our **o**_____ way instead of **G**_____'s way.

• God has made the punishment we deserve fall on **J**_____.

Imagine a sheep that has wandered off and got lost. Maybe it's trapped on a high ledge, or caught in a bush. It <u>can't</u> save itself. It needs to be **rescued**.

You and I are like that sheep. We all sin, and that stops us from being friends with God. We <u>can't</u> save ourselves. We need to be **rescued**.

---

*Copy all the **red letters** (in order) to see something wonderful.*

_ _ _ _ _ _ _ _

_ _ _ _ _ _ _ _ _ _

THINK + PRAY

When Jesus died, He took the punishment we deserve, so that we can be <u>rescued</u> from our sins and can be friends with God. Have you put your trust in Jesus to rescue you? No?—then ask Him to. Yes?—then thank Him right now!
If you're not sure how Jesus rescues us, check out 'God's Rescue Plan' after Day 21.

Welcome back to the book of **2 Kings**. Crack the code for a quick reminder of what's happened so far to the kingdoms of **Israel** and **Judah**...

ISRAEL

- God _ _ _ _ _ _ them that they must love and obey Him.

- They _ _ _ _ _ _ _ God's warnings.

- So they were

_ _ _ _ _ _ _ _ _ by the Assyrians and taken away from their country.

JUDAH

- God _ _ _ _ _ _ them that they must love and obey Him.

- If they _ _ _ _ _ _ _ God's warnings they would be

_ _ _ _ _ _ _ _ by their enemies (as Israel were) and taken away from their country.

- Last time, we met King Hezekiah, who was the <u>best</u> king Judah ever had.
- But his son Manasseh was an **evil** king, who made God very angry (2 Kings 21v6).
- And Hezekiah's grandson Amon was also an evil king, just like Manasseh.

Wow! Does that mean God carried out His warning?

Yes! Manasseh and Amon <u>ignored</u> God's warnings, so God did what He said He would. He allowed their enemies to <u>capture</u> the people of Judah.

More on the next page...

A = ■   D = ■   I = ◆   O = ★   T = ✚   W = ◣

B = ■   E = ●   L = ◆   P = ★   U = ✚   Y = ◣

C = ■   G = ●   N = ✳   R = ★   V = ✚

Shape Code

In the next few days we'll read the sad story of Judah being attacked and captured. But they had one more <u>good</u> king first...

READ
2 Kings 22v1-2

Who was the new king? (v1)

J_____

How old was he when he became king? (v1)

_____ **years old**

What kind of king was Josiah? (v2)
a) An evil king like his father **Amon**.
b) An evil king like his grandfather **Manasseh**.
c) A good king like his ancestor **David**.

 2 Kings 22v1-2

How old are you? _____

Which of these do you hope to do when you're older? ○Circle○ your answers and add more of your own.

Drive a car   Get a job   Be a lion tamer
Get married
Be a pop star   Be famous
Play sport for   Be a mum or dad
your country

 THINK SPOT
When you grow up you'll have lots of <u>choices</u> to make—such as what job to do, or whether to get married. But you <u>don't</u> have to wait until you're older to make the important choice that Josiah made!

Josiah chose to __ __ __ __ God and __ __ __ __ Him. And Josiah lived that way all his life.

PRAY
What about you? How do <u>you</u> want to live your life? Think carefully—then talk to God about your answer.

DAY 57 A BOOK IS FOUND

 2 Kings 22v3-13

Yesterday, we saw that God <u>warned</u> the people of Judah to love and obey Him. If they didn't, God would allow them to be <u>captured</u> by their enemies.

We know that God was going to carry out His warning soon. But **Josiah** <u>didn't</u> know that—<u>yet!</u>

In today's reading, good King Josiah is now 26 years old. He sent Shaphan, his secretary (assistant), to see how the temple repairs were getting on. Shaphan came back with some news...

Hilkiah the priest has given me a book.

It was found in the temple.

The book would have been written on a scroll. It was probably part of the Old Testament.

READ
2 Kings 22v10-13

What did Josiah do when he heard God's words in the book? (v11)

Josiah
t_____
his clothes.

Why was Josiah so upset? (v13)
a) He knew that God was angry.
b) He knew that the people hadn't obeyed God's words in the book.

<u>Both</u> answers are correct! Josiah knew that God was angry because the people hadn't obeyed Him.

Josiah's father and grandfather hadn't cared about God's words. But **Josiah** was very different. He knew that God's words were hugely important. And he knew that God would do what He had warned. *More about that tomorrow...*

THINK + PRAY

How do <u>you</u> react to God's words in the Bible?
• Do you rush through XTB as fast as you can?
• Do you sometimes skip the hard bits?
• Do you ask God to speak to you through His Word, and to show you how He wants you to live?
Think carefully about each question, and then talk to God about your answers.

DAY 58 GOD'S CHARACTER

Josiah had just heard God's words read to him from a book that had been found in the temple. So he sent his men to see a prophetess (God's messenger) called **Huldah** to find out more...

READ
2 Kings 22v14-20

Huldah had a message for Josiah from **God**: "I will bring **trouble** to this place and to the people living here. The people of Judah have made me **angry** by all the idols they have made. Tell the king of Judah that because he **tore** his robes and **wept** in my presence he will be buried in peace. The punishment I am bringing will **not** come until **after** his death."

Find the <u>blue words</u> in the wordsearch.
Some are backwards!

J	U	W	E	P	T	T	O	N
D	G	E	M	A	N	G	R	Y
E	R	O	T	E	N	G	O	D
R	E	T	F	A	T	G	R	A
T	R	O	U	B	L	E	C	E

The <u>leftover letters</u> from the wordsearch spell **two words**. *Copy those letters here to see what they are.*

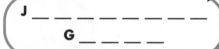

J _ _ _ _ _ _ _ _

G _ _ _ _ _

Judgement
God was going to punish the people of Judah for turning away from Him.

Grace
God showed grace (HUGE kindness) to Josiah. He promised not to punish the people while Josiah was alive.

These verses show us two sides of God's character. They seem quite different, but both have to be there— like the two sides of the same coin...

Judgement
God makes sure that sin is punished.

Grace
God's HUGE kindness to people who don't deserve it.

THINK + PRAY

Think of some ways that God has shown His **grace** to you. *(eg: answering your prayers, sending Jesus to save you from your sins...)* Thank God for these things now.

My mum has just had a party. She spent ages cleaning up first! What was the last party <u>you</u> went to?

2 Kings 23 tells us of some <u>cleaning up</u> King Josiah did, before a fantastic <u>party</u>...

CLEANING UP
Take the first letter of each pic to see some of the cleaning up.

- Josiah and the people  __ __ __ __ __ __ __ __ to keep God's commands. (v1-3)

- Anything used to worship __ __ __ __ __ __ __ __ gods (idols) was cleared out of the temple. (v4-7)

- The __ __ __ __ __ __ __ used to worship idols were destroyed. (v8-20)

PARTY TIME
Then it was party time! Their celebration was called __ __ __ __ __ __ __ __ __ .

READ
2 Kings 23v21-23

Did you know?
Passover was a time to remember a great Rescue— when God rescued the Israelites from Egypt. *You can read about the first ever Passover meal in Exodus 12v1-14.*

THINK+PRAY

Can <u>you</u> be like Josiah and his people?
First: Have a 'clean up' by saying sorry to God for the times you have let Him down this week. Ask Him to help you to change.
Next: Think of a way to celebrate an even greater Rescue—the fact that Jesus has rescued you from your sins. How can you celebrate?
- Write a list of thank yous to God on your XTB Pad?
- Sing a song thanking God?
- Make a cake or biscuits to eat at a 'thank you meal'?
- Or do <u>all</u> of these!

DAY 60 GOD'S JUDGEMENT

 xtb 2 Kings 23v25–24v20

There was never a king like Josiah.

He obeyed God with all his heart, soul and strength. (2 Kings 23v25)

But God was still angry with the people of Judah.

I will reject Judah and Jerusalem!

After Josiah died, his son Jehoahaz became king.

But he was an <u>evil</u> king!

The next king was called Jehoiakim.

He was an <u>evil</u> king too!

Jehoiakim was followed by Jehoiachin!

He was another <u>evil</u> king!

Then Nebuchadnezzar, king of Babylon, captured Jerusalem.

–just as God had said.

Nebuchadnezzar removed all the treasures from the temple.

–just as God had said.

Nebuchadnezzar also took the king, his army and most of the people back to Babylon.

–just as God had said.

Then Nebuchadnezzar made Zedekiah the new king of Jerusalem…

READ
2 Kings 24v18-20

What kind of king was Zedekiah? (v19)

A good king / An evil king

<u>Why</u> did all these things happen to Judah and Jerusalem? (v20)

a) Because Nebuchadnezzar hated them.

b) Because God was angry with them.

c) The Bible doesn't tell us.

THINK + PRAY

Do you remember the two sides of God's character? Judgement and grace. Today we've seen God's **judgement**—just as He said it would happen. Does God's judgement scare you? It should! **But** if you've put your trust in Jesus then <u>He</u> has rescued you, and you have nothing to be scared of. That's grace! Talk to God about this now.

GOD IS WITH US

The **temple** in Jerusalem was a magnificent building, beautifully decorated and full of gold. But that's <u>not</u> why it was special.

The temple was special because it reminded the Israelites of something very important. *Crack the code to see what that was.*

→ ↕ ⇦ ↓ ▽ ▷ ↓ ◀ ↑ ▶ ▽

— — — — — — — — — — —

The temple reminded God's people that **He** was with them.

⇨ = A   ⇦ = D   ⇪ = E   → = G   ↑ = H
↓ = I   ↖ = J   ↗ = K   ↘ = M   ↔ = N   ↕ = O
△ = R   ▽ = S   ◀ = T   ▶ = U   ▷ = W

BUT the king of Jerusalem (Zedekiah) rebelled against the king of Babylon (Nebuchadnezzar). So Nebuchadnezzar sent his army to Jerusalem...

READ
2 Kings 25v8-12

What happened to the temple? (v9)

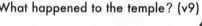

When God's temple was burned down, it was a sign that God was <u>not</u> with His people any more. He had rejected them—just as He had warned them. The people were taken away to exile (to live in Babylon).

What a sad end! But it's not quite the end of 2 Kings. 37 years later, King Jehoiachin (a captive in Babylon) was freed from prison (v27-30).

Um... So what??

God had promised <u>not</u> to wipe out the family line of King David. (2 Sam 7v16) One day, someone from that family would be born as God's perfect King. One of His names would be 'Immanuel' which means 'God with us'!

This perfect King was

↗ ↓ ↔ → ↖ ⇨ ▽ ▶ ▽

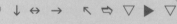

— — — — — — — — —

PRAY Thank God for keeping His promise to send our perfect King.

A LETTER FROM GOD

Jerusalem had been captured by King Nebuchadnezzar, and the Israelites taken away to live in Babylon. Then the Israelites were sent a <u>letter</u> It was written by one of God's prophets (messengers). *Use yesterday's code to see his name* .

↖ ⇨ △ ⇨ ↘ ↓ ⇨ ↑

— — — — — — — —

Although it was Jeremiah who <u>wrote</u> the letter, the message was from **God** ...

READ
Jeremiah 29v4-10

<u>Who</u> had taken the people away from their country? (*It's called* **exile**.) (v4)
a) God
b) Nebuchadnezzar
c) Jeremiah

It was **God** who sent the people away, and He used Nebuchadnezzar to do it.

What were the people to do now? (v5-7) (Circle) *the correct answers.*

Build houses   Have children
Plant gardens   Fight back
    Don't listen to lies
Watch TV   Dig a tunnel
Write letters   Marry
    Pray for the city they lived in

It was God who took His people into exile. Now they had to accept it, and settle down there.

But God also promised to bring His people back home! How long would they have to wait? (v10)

 _____ **years**

THINK SPOT The Israelites <u>deserved</u> to be in exile. It was their punishment for turning away from God. But God didn't **forget** His people. He got Jeremiah to write them a letter. And He gave them a wonderful promise. (*More about that tomorrow* .)

THINK + PRAY God never forgets <u>you</u> either! The whole Bible is like a huge letter from God to you. What do you like best about God's letter, the Bible? Thank Him for it now.

DAY 63 GOD'S GENEROUS PROMISE

 xtb Jeremiah 29v10-14

We're reading God's letter to the Israelites who were living in Babylon. God has just promised to bring His people back home again. Now He has some other wonderful things to say to them...

READ
Jeremiah 29v10-14

(Circle) *the correct answers.*

- When 70 years are over I will **bring/send/post** you back home. (v10)
- I have **bad/good/boring** plans for you. (v11)
- You will **call/curtsy/cry** on me and I will **ignore/listen/talk** to you. (v12)
- You will seek me, and find me, when you seek me with all your **money/telescopes/heart**. (v13)

Now fit your answers into the puzzle. The <u>yellow boxes</u> will spell a new word.

THINK + PRAY

God loves to be generous! He gives us so many good things. Jot some of them down on your **XTB Writing Pad**—and then write a huge **'THANKYOU'** underneath. (*If you're stuck for ideas, there are some below.*)

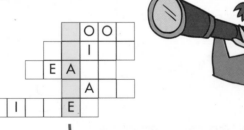

God looks after the world we live in; He gives us the food, water and air we need to live; He listens to our prayers; He gives us homes to live in and people to take care of us; He sent His own Son to rescue us; and much, much more...

Jeremiah
29v12-13

Have you ever played 'Hide and Seek'? Did you ever choose such a good hiding place that you couldn't be found???

There are **five letters** hiding in this puzzle. Find them by crossing out all the letters that appear **two** or **three times**.

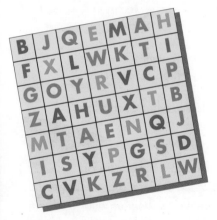

B	J	Q	E	M	A	H
F	X	L	W	K	T	I
G	O	Y	R	V	C	P
Z	A	H	U	X	T	B
M	T	A	E	N	Q	J
I	S	Y	P	G	S	D
C	V	K	Z	R	L	W

Now copy the hidden letters (in order) to spell a five-letter word.

— — — — —

In yesterday's reading, God told His people to **seek** Him. But God isn't hiding—He **wants** to be found!!!

READ
Jeremiah 29v12-13

THINK SPOT

'Seeking' God doesn't mean looking for Him with a telescope! How can <u>you</u> seek and find God?

THINK + PRAY

The best way to find God is by reading His book to us, the Bible, and then praying about what we read. It also helps to meet with other Christians (maybe at church or a Christian group) so that we can help each other to get to know God better. List three ways that you can seek God this week:

1 _____

2 _____

3 _____

Ask God to help you to find Him and get to know Him better as you do these things.

DAY 65 GETTING TO KNOW GOD

xtb — John 14v6-11

Choose some words to describe **Jesus**. Try and think of at least three.

loving

Now crack the code to see something Jesus said about Himself.

Anyone who has

`■ ■ ■ ■ ✕` = N

_ _ _ _ _

`◆ K ▯ ▯ ▬ ✚`

has seen the _ _ _ _ _ _

Flag Code

Flag	Letter
	= A
	= E
◆	= F
	= H
✕	= M
	= N
✚	= R
■	= S
▯	= T

Yesterday we saw that God wants us to find Him. Today we're jumping into John's Gospel to see what Jesus said about how we can find and know God. In these verses, Jesus calls God 'the Father'...

READ
John 14v6-11

<u>Who</u> do we look at if we want to see God the Father? (v9)

Wow! If we want to see what God is like, we can look at Jesus.

THINK + PRAY

Look again at your list of words at the beginning of the page. These words show us what God, our perfect Father, is like. Use those words in a prayer to thank God for being like this. Now ask God to help you to get to know Him better and better as you learn more about Jesus.

TIME FOR MORE?

Have you read all 65 days of XTB?
Well done if you have!

How often do you use XTB?
- Every day?
- Nearly every day?
- Two or three times a week?
- Now and then?

You can use XTB at any time...

In the morning.

At bedtime.

When you get back from school.

When do <u>you</u> read XTB?

XTB comes out every three months. If you've been using it every day, or nearly every day, that's great! You may still have a few weeks to wait before you get the next issue of XTB. But don't worry!—that's what the extra readings are for...

EXTRA READINGS
The next four pages contain extra Bible readings about the names and titles for Jesus. If you read one each day, they will take you 26 days. Or you may want to read two or three each day. Or just pick a few to try. Whichever suits you best. There's a cracking wordsearch to solve too...

Drop us a line...
Why not write in and tell us what you think of XTB:
—What do you like best?
—Was there something you didn't understand?
—And any ideas for how we can make it better!

Write to: XTB, The Good Book Company, Blenheim House, 1 Blenheim Road, Epsom, Surrey, KT19 9AP, UK
or e-mail me: alison@thegoodbook.co.uk

The extra readings start on the next page

NAMES AND TITLES FOR JESUS

As we saw on Day 53, the prophet Isaiah knew some of the names for Jesus hundreds of years <u>before</u> Jesus was born! In these extra readings we're going to discover many more...

Jesus
These extra readings come from many different books in the Bible. Each one looks at a name or title for Jesus, and explains what that name means.

The ideas in the box will help you as you read the verses.

PRAY Ask God to help you to understand what you read.

READ Read the Bible verses, and fill in the missing word in the puzzle.

THINK Think about what you have just read. Try to work out one main thing the writer is saying.

PRAY Thank God for what you have learnt about Him.

There are 26 Bible readings on the next three pages. Part of each reading has been printed for you—but with a word missing. Fill in the missing words as you read the verses. Then see if you can find them all in the wordsearch below. Some are written backwards—or diagonally!

If you get stuck, check the answers at the end of Reading 26.

B	E	A	R	E	S	U	R	R	E	C	T	I	O	N
E	R	D	E	V	A	S	W	A	Y	L	M	A	S	H
G	R	E	E	N	V	O	B	E	L	I	E	V	E	A
I	I	S	A	D	I	C	X	T	B	G	O	O	R	T
N	S	T	A	R	O	H	F	A	T	H	E	R	V	I
N	B	M	A	L	U	R	E	D	B	T	S	T	E	M
I	X	T	B	P	R	I	N	C	E	L	A	S	A	M
N	A	M	E	R	U	S	H	V	A	N	V	R	O	A
G	A	T	D	G	A	T	E	I	N	T	E	I	L	N
X	T	F	O	U	N	D	U	N	X	T	B	F	S	U
B	W	H	O	B	I	B	L	E	Y	A	D	O	T	E
Y	T	H	G	I	M	W	O	N	D	E	R	F	U	L

1 ☐ **Read Matthew 1v18-21**

*The name **Jesus** means 'God Saves'. It tells us who Jesus is: He is **God**; and what Jesus does: He **saves** us from our sins.*

'You are to give Him the name Jesus, because He will **s _ _ _** His people from their sins.' (v21)

2 ☐ **Read Matthew 1v22-25**

*Jesus was also given the name **Immanuel** (sometimes written as 'Emmanuel'). This name means 'God with us'.*

'He will be called **I _ _ _ _ _ _ _ _** .' (v23)

3 ☐ **Read Luke 2v11-14**

*The angels told the shepherds that Jesus, their **Saviour** (Rescuer), had been born.*

'This very day in David's town your **S _ _ _ _ _ _ _** was born—Christ the Lord!' (v11)

4 ☐ **Read Mark 1v1**

*Jesus is often called **Jesus Christ**. This isn't His surname! 'Christ' is a Greek name meaning 'God's chosen King'.*

'The beginning of the gospel (good news) about Jesus **C _ _ _ _ _ _** , the Son of God.' (v1)

5 ☐ **Read John 1v40-42**

***Christ** is a Greek name. The same name in the Hebrew language is **Messiah**.*

'We have **f _ _ _ _** the Messiah.' (v41)

6 ☐ **Read John 20v30-31**

*Jesus was a human being, like you and me. But He is also God! The Bible often calls Jesus '**the Son of God**'.*

'These have been written in order that you may **b _ _ _ _ _ _** that Jesus is the Christ, the Son of God.' (v31)

7 ☐ **Read Luke 19v1-10**

*Jesus sometimes called Himself the '**Son of Man**'. He said that He came to look for and rescue lost people.*

'The Son of Man came to seek and to **s _ _ _** the lost.' (v10)

8 ☐ **Read Matthew 21v1-9**

*God had promised that someone from King David's family would be King for ever. Jesus was that promised '**Son of David**'.*

'Hosanna to the Son of David! Blessed is He who comes in the **n _ _ _** of the Lord!' (v9)

9 ☐ **Read Matthew 21v10-11**

*Jesus was born in Bethlehem, but He grew up in the town of Nazareth. So He was sometimes called '**Jesus of Nazareth**'.*

' "**W _ _** is this?" the people asked.' (v10)

10 ☐ **Read John 6v32-35**

There are seven 'I AM' sayings in John's Gospel, when Jesus said "I am…". In the first one, Jesus says He is like bread that gives eternal life.
'I am the **b** _ _ _ _ of life.' (v35)

11 ☐ **Read John 8v12**

The devil wants people to be lost in darkness—without God. But Jesus brings light!
'I am the **L** _ _ _ _ of the world.' (v12)

12 ☐ **Read John 10v7-10**

Jesus is like a gate or door. He is the only way to be rescued from our sins and live for ever in heaven.

'I am the **g** _ _ _ . Whoever enters by me will be saved.' (v9)

13 ☐ **Read John 10v11-15**

Jesus is like a perfect shepherd. He loves His sheep (His people), and even died to rescue them!
'I am the **g** _ _ _ shepherd.' (v11)

14 ☐ **Read John 11v25-26**

Jesus is the only one who gives eternal life. If someone who believes in Jesus dies, he will be raised to life again. This is called resurrection.
'I am the
r _ _ _ _ _ _ _ _ _ _ _ _
and the life.' (v25)

15 ☐ **Read John 14v5-6**

Jesus is the <u>only</u> way to be right with God, and to live with Him for ever in heaven.
'I am the **w** _ _ , the truth and the life. No one comes to the Father except through me.' (v6)

16 ☐ **Read John 15v1-5**

Followers of Jesus grow to live the way He wants them to— like branches on a vine grow fruit.
'I am the **v** _ _ _ , and you are the branches.' (v5)

17 ☐ **Read John 1v29**

Jesus died to take the punishment for our sin—like a perfect lamb, dying in our place.
'There is the **L** _ _ _ of God, who takes away the sin of the world.' (v29)

18 ☐ **Read Mark 10v42-45**

*Even though Jesus is our King, He came to serve people, and to die as our ransom (which means paying the cost to rescue us). He is our **Servant King**!*
'The Son of Man did not come to be served, but to **s** _ _ _ _ , and to give His life as a ransom for many.' (v45)

19 ☐ **Read Isaiah 9v6-7**

Hundreds of years before Jesus was born, Isaiah gave Him some very special titles. The first one tells us that Jesus shows us the best way to live.
'He will be called
W _ _ _ _ _ _ _ _
Counsellor...' (v6)

20 ☐ **Read Isaiah 9v6-7**

Jesus is God! He is mighty and powerful.
'He will be called Wonderful
Counsellor, M _ _ _ _ _ God...'
(v6)

21 ☐ **Read Isaiah 9v6-7**

Jesus is everlasting! He has always existed and always will.
'He will be called Wonderful
Counsellor, Mighty God,
Everlasting F _ _ _ _ _ ...' (v6)

22 ☐ **Read Isaiah 9v6-7 (again!)**

Jesus brings us peace with God.
'He will be called Wonderful
Counsellor, Mighty God, Everlasting
Father, P _ _ _ _ _ of Peace.'
(v6)

23 ☐ **Read John 1v1-3**

John starts his Gospel by telling us that Jesus is 'the Word', and that He made everything.
'From the very
b _ _ _ _ _ _ _ _ _ the Word
was with God.' (v2)

24 ☐ **Read Revelation 22v13**

The last book in the Bible tells us that Jesus is the beginning and end of all things. Most versions say 'Alpha and Omega', which are the first and last letters in the Greek alphabet.
'I am the Alpha and the Omega, the
F _ _ _ _ and the Last, the
Beginning and the End.' (v13)

25 ☐ **Read Revelation 22v16**

In the book of Revelation, Jesus also tells us that He is like a bright star shining in the morning.
'I am the bright Morning
S _ _ _ .' (v16)

26 ☐ **Read Hebrews 13v8**

Jesus never changes. Everything we have read about Him in these extra readings will be true for ever!
'Jesus Christ is the same yesterday,
t _ _ _ _ and forever.' (v8)

WHAT NEXT?

XTB comes out every three months. Each issue contains 65 full XTB pages, plus 26 days of extra readings. By the time you've used them all, the next issue of XTB will be available.

ISSUE TWELVE OF XTB: End to End

Issue Twelve of XTB explores the books of John, Daniel, Nehemiah and Revelation.

- Read about the very first Easter in **John**'s Gospel.
- Meet **Daniel**, one of the young men captured by King Nebuchadnezzar.
- Find out how the Israelites came home in **Nehemiah**
- And explore the last book in the Bible—**Revelation**.

Available from your local Christian bookshop—or:
www.thegoodbook.co.uk
www.thegoodbook.com

Look out for these three seasonal editions of XTB:
Christmas Unpacked, Easter Unscrambled and *Summer Signposts*. Available now.

XTB Joke Page

What do frogs wear on the beach?
Open-toad sandals!

Who is the boss of the hankies?
The handkerchief!!

What do you get if a banana hits a strawberry?
Fruit punch!

What do you get if you cross a centipede with a parrot?
A walkie-talkie!

All sent in by Helena Stone and Jennie Thornborough.

Why was 6 afraid of 7?
Because 7 ate 9!

Knock, knock.
Who's there?
Who
Who who?
You're an owl too!

Both sent in by Mitchell Roberts.

Do <u>you</u> know any good jokes?
—send them in and they might appear in XTB!

Do you have any questions?
...about anything you've read in XTB?
—send them in and we'll do our best to answer them.

Write to: XTB, The Good Book Company, at the address on the inside cover **or e-mail me:** alison@thegoodbook.co.uk